An Age of Opportunity

An Age of Opportunity

INTENTIONAL MINISTRY BY, WITH, AND FOR OLDER ADULTS

Richard H. Gentzler, Jr.

DISCIPLESHIP
RESOURCES

ISBNs

978-0-88177-903-5 (print)
978-0-88177-904-2 (mobi)
978-0-88177-905-9 (ePub)

AN AGE OF OPPORTUNITY:
INTENTIONAL MINISTRY BY, WITH, AND FOR OLDER ADULTS

Printed in the United States of America.

DR903

This book is dedicated to

My best friend and wife, Marilyn;

My wonderful children, Dr. Richard III (Emily) and Elizabeth, Esq. (Jennifer); and

My exceptional grandchildren, Katie and Henry.

Contents

Acknowledgments

I am grateful to the hundreds of church leaders (both clergy and laity) and congregations throughout The United Methodist Church, who, over the years, have given me greater understanding and insight into the challenges of aging, the needs of older adults, and who are themselves actively engaged in intentional ministry by, with, and for older adults.

To Kent McNish, executive director, and Charles Hewgley, board president, and the board of directors of the Golden Cross Foundation of the Tennessee Conference, who gave their unwavering support and approval for the development of ENCORE Ministries. To the Rev. James Robinson, chair, and members of the ENCORE Ministries Advisory Team for their ongoing advice and visionary leadership. And, to Shirley Vaughn, chair, and members of the Tennessee Conference Committee on Older Adult Ministries for their faithful efforts in resourcing the needs of congregations in older-adult ministries.

To Grace Smith, executive director of the Council on Aging of Middle Tennessee, to the staff, to my colleagues on the board of directors, and to the hundreds of volunteers who make a positive impact in the lives of older people and their families throughout middle Tennessee.

To the Rev. Dr. William Randolph, director of pastoral care at Longwood at Oakmont, Pennsylvania, and former director of the Office on Aging and Older Adult Ministries for Discipleship Ministries, for his friendship, encouragement and support in the writing of this book. To Joseph Crowe, project manager at Discipleship Resources for his hard work in guiding the publication of this book, and to Cheryl Capshaw, copy editor, for her amazing skill in bringing clarity and readability to this book.

Foreword

For years, *Designing an Older Adult Ministry* was the workhorse book that the office I had served recommended to almost every church leader who contacted us for older-adult ministry resources. It was perfect for clergy and laity who were passionate about older-adult ministry, but did not know how to get started. It was the single best resource for how to begin, develop, and expand older-adult ministry in a variety of church settings, worldwide. As great a resource as it still is, it was written nearly twenty years ago before Dr. Richard Gentzler wrote his visionary book, *Aging and Ministry in the Twenty-First Century and Beyond*, which predictively described the great wave of change emerging in aging and older-adult ministry, as baby boomers become a part of the sixty-five and older population. In other words, *Designing an Older Adult Ministry*, while still a great book for traditional older-adult ministry, did not focus upon how to minister to, for, and with, baby boomers, who are now a part of the church's older-adult population. With this end in mind, I specifically asked him to update *Designing an Older Adult Ministry*. *An Age of Opportunity* is the result.

I believe that Dr. Gentzler is the only person who has both the personal experience and the insight to write a book like *An Age of Opportunity*. I was aware I was asking him to do the near-impossible task of writing a book to cover ministry with four current generations of older adults, including baby boomers, a group that often does not consider itself old. In answering the challenge, Dr. Gentzler, has written a powerful new resource for church leaders.

An Age of Opportunity addresses issues such as ageism in the church and opportunities that leaders miss when they view ministry as ministry *to* older adults instead of ministry *with* older adults. Dr. Gentzler discusses "difference-making opportunities" such as caregiver support, identify re-formation in retirement, widowhood, elder abuse, poverty, and grief.

An Age of Opportunity fits neatly into a three-volume set of books that will serve church volunteers and staff for a long time to come: *An Age of Opportunity*, *Designing an Older Adult Ministry*, and *Aging and Ministry in the Twenty-First Century and Beyond*. Leaders can now use *Designing an Older Adult Ministry* as a sourcebook for how to engage with the oldest of older adults. Now with *An Age of Opportunity*, they can discover how to grow their ministry into a truly spectacular, creative, and visionary model that will serve the church.

—Rev. Dr. William Randolph
Former Director of Aging and Older Adult Ministries
Discipleship Ministries, The United Methodist Church
Director of Pastoral Care at Longwood
in Oakmont, Pennsylvania

Introduction—An Age of Opportunity

"So even to old age and gray hairs, O God, do not forsake me, until I proclaim your might to all the generations to come."

—Psalm 71:18

Age Is Opportunity

But why, you ask me, should this tale be told
To men grown old, or who are growing old?
It is too late! Ah, nothing is too late
Till the tired heart shall cease to palpitate.
Cato learned Greek at eighty; Sophocles
Wrote his grand Oedipus, and Simonides
Bore off the prize of verse from his compeers,
When each had numbered more than four-
score years,
And Theophrastus, at fourscore and ten,

Had but begun in "Characters of Men,"
Chaucer, at Woodstock with the nightingales,
At sixty wrote the Canterbury Tales;
Goethe at Weimar, toiling to the last,
Completed Faust when eighty years were past.
These are indeed exceptions; but they show
How far the gulf-stream of our youth may
flow. . . .
The night hath not yet come; we are not quite
Cut off from labor by the failing light;
Something remains for us to do or dare;
Even the oldest tree some fruit may bear. . . .
For age is opportunity no less
Than youth itself, though in another dress,
And as the evening twilight fades away
The sky is filled with stars, invisible by day.
Henry Wadsworth Longfellow
From *Morituri Salutamus*

One of the great success stories of the twentieth century and continuing into the twenty-first century has been the increased longevity of our population. Until rather recently in human history, very few people grew old. Most people did not reach old age. They died! And many people died at a relatively young age. Women died at a young age from childbirth, from the hardships of frontier life, and from various untreatable diseases. Men died as a result of warfare, from the strenuous labor of clearing land, from agricultural or mining accidents, and from diseases and illnesses. Our modern longevity revolution is truly something to celebrate.

In 1900, the population age sixty-five and over was 3.1 million (about four percent of the total population). According to the U.S. Census, the population age sixty-five and over has increased from 36.6 million in 2005 to 47.8 million people in 2015 (a thirty percent increase) and is projected to increase to 82.3 million by 2040. The 85 and older population is expected to grow from 6.7 million in 2015 to 14.6 million in 2040; and those over age 100 now total almost 77,000. About one in seven, or 14.9 percent of the population is an older American (*A Profile of Older Americans*, pages 1–3).[1]

Tremendous advances in scientific discoveries, medical technology, health care, economic security, job safety, the delivery of supportive services, and a host of other variables have profoundly altered the experience of aging for the better. Today, 10,000 people turn sixty-five years of age every day in the United States, about one person every eight seconds.

According to the U. S. Census, new detailed estimates show the nation's median age—the age where half of the population is younger and the other half older—rose from 35.1 years in 2000 to about 38 years today. The baby boom generation (boomers) is largely responsible for this trend because of the large number of births during the period of 1946–1964 (U.S. Census).[2]

We all know that older adults are living longer, but there is more to it than that. Older adults who are not encumbered by ageism are transforming what it means to be sixty, seventy, eighty, ninety, and even one hundred and older. They are reinventing the idea of old age and doing it in ways that benefit their congregations, their communities, their health, their families; and they are setting an example for succeeding generations.

Growing older today is a time of opportunity. To be sure, old age is a blessed gift; and with the help of modern science and good health care, the biblical expression of "three score and ten" has been upgraded considerably.

These exciting improvements for older Americans and their families have created both new opportunities and new challenges. Although more people than ever before will experience an extended phase of life in which they will be seen as "aged" or "older," it has become less clear what aging might mean or what older people could contribute to society other than as consumers of health care. To regard aging as a pathological process, even when it comes with illness or disability, means to ignore the basic dignity and creative potential of older adults.

Since we live in a society that views aging as decline, a disease, or dependency, and places the value of people's worth on their productivity or beauty, it is not easy to discern what it means to grow old. Our culture is preoccupied with being, acting, and looking young. Because of a fear of aging, our society does not validate growing old. As a result, our cultural view of aging prevents people of all ages from seeing that the challenges of growing old are as bountiful as are the problems among older adults. Every age and stage of life has its own unique challenges and transitions that are filled with potentialities and crises.

Unfortunately, even among our congregations, many churches have not captured the full vision for intentional ministry by, with, and for older adults. The dominant tendencies to define people as "aged," "elderly," or "old" when they have reached a certain chronological age and to believe that church vitality can be realized only with growing numbers of young people discounts the blessing and potential of these years. Further, dismissing the faith and life experiences of older adults and regarding older adults as embodiments of "a past life" prevent the integration of older adults in the normal life of the church.

While churches engage much energy in reaching and enhancing the faith experiences of children, youth, and young adults, and do so for obvious reasons, they often fail to develop the spiritual development and full potential of people at midlife and beyond. By not supporting and equipping the faith development and spiritual growth of older adults, churches are not only hindering the full potential of older people but are failing the spiritual well-being of people of all ages. The church is called to make disciples of Jesus Christ. Christian discipleship knows no age boundaries. As apostle Paul wrote: "for in Christ Jesus you are all children of God through faith. . . .There is no longer Jew or Greek, there is no longer slave or free, there is no longer male and female; for all of you are one in Christ Jesus" (Galatians 3:26, 28). Perhaps if Paul were writing this today, he might also include, "There is no longer young or old; we are all one in Christ."

It is helpful to keep in mind that age sixty-five no longer signals the onset of late life. People who are now sixty-five generally are healthier, wealthier, and better educated than their age cohorts of previous generations. Aging is no longer synonymous with death. Churches that recognize both the gifts and strengths of older adults as well as the challenges they face will be better able to envision God's purpose for long life among older adults. Congregations that are open-minded and discerning are experiencing this time as an age of opportunity. People who are living longer have the opportunity to grow in Christ and faith maturity. Churches have opportunities for Christian discipleship by, with, and for older adults through intentional ministry.

The purpose of this book is to provide local church leaders (both clergy and lay) with tools and vision needed to create intentional ministries by, with, and for older adults that can, and will, enhance the spiritual growth and well-being of people of all ages. The church is beginning to recognize that there are vast numbers of older people in its membership. It is becoming aware of its indebtedness to them for the leadership, support, service, and faith that has made the church of today possible. The church is uniquely positioned to help older adults respond to the challenges of aging; to see the tremendous potentialities in the lives of older adult for making the church and community better; and to assist older people as they experience new meaning and purpose in their later lives.

We are living in an age of opportunity. While our health care and medical institutions have moved from simply saving lives to prolonging lives, the church has an important role in optimizing lives. We need to get rid of outdated stereotypes about aging and spark new solutions and new directions for ministry. We need to first challenge our own outdated attitudes and stereotypes about aging, and we have to create a new mindset around aging and graying congregations and develop solutions for reimaging congregational vitality.

Three questions can help guide church leaders in ministry with older adults:

1. How does your church harness the creativity, wisdom, experience, and faith that exists in the hearts and minds of older members?
2. What are ways your church offers opportunities for older adults to find meaning and purpose in the later years?
3. What are ways your church provides opportunities for older adults to grow in faith and in a loving relationship with God through Jesus Christ?

Each chapter in this book provides the reader with insight and helpful information for creating and sustaining intentional ministry with boomers and our older-adult population. Chapter 1 explains why there is a growing need for an intentional ministry by, with, and for older adults in our churches. Chapter 2 provides the reader with a brief reference in understanding the aging process, which can serve as a useful reference for the development of intentional ministry. Chapter 3 examines aging in light of our understanding of religion and spirituality and provides helpful insight into the role of the church in the spiritual well-being of older adults. Chapter 4 specifically addresses the boomer generation and identifies leading-edge boomers as the new generation of older adults. Chapter 5 looks at starting and sustaining intentional ministry by, with, and for older adults. Chapter 6 provides organizing principles for intentional ministry in the local church, while Chapter 7 provides information about organizing for intentional ministry on the judicatory level. Chapter 8 identifies congregational ministry ideas, and Chapter 9 provides additional models for ministry by local churches. The final chapter, Chapter 10, looks at a few of the many aging trends that congregations will need to consider for future directions in ministry.

Following Chapter 10 are several helpful appendixes that provide additional resource information. Finally, there is also an annotated resource list for further reading and study.

An Age of Opportunity can be used as a quick-reference for church leaders looking for tools, resources, and best practices. It includes information based on various experiences in building local leadership and solving specific challenges related to aging and the church.

My goal and prayer is that local churches will realize this era as an age of opportunity for creating new ministries with boomers and older adults so that they may grow as disciples of Jesus Christ and, along with people of all ages, help build the kingdom of God.

CHAPTER 1

Why Older-Adult Ministries?

"You shall rise before the aged, and defer to the old; and you shall fear your God; I am the Lord."

—LEVITICUS 19:32

Our world is aging. And, despite all that has been written in recent years about aging, aging itself is a relatively new phenomenon. Life expectancy in 1900 was forty-seven years. By 2015, life expectancy in the United States had increased to nearly seventy-nine years, more than thirty years longer than in 1900 *(A Profile of Older Americans: 2016,* Administration on Aging, 2).[1] For the first time in our nation's history, we are becoming a country of older people.

Medical science has had a tremendous impact on the changing age demographics in our country. Changes in infant mortality have especially been significant in escalating the rise in life expectancy. But better health care, safety precautions in industry, economic progress, and the delivery of supportive services have all played important roles in increased life expectancy.

When we look around our world, we can see that work, housing, retirement, economic and social resources, transportation, technology, health care, and even education and intergenerational relationships are all being transformed by a population that is aging. Our "youth oriented" culture is fast giving way to the possibilities of a new and exciting "elder culture." But what about the church? While it may be true that many societal institutions have been preparing for and gaining ground on the needs of an aging population, unfortunately, not many congregations are fully prepared, nor are church leaders properly equipped, to deal with graying congregations.

The image of an older congregation is often seen by both clergy and laity as outdated, closed-minded and holding steadfastly to tradition. Some believe that graying congregations are a hindrance to church growth and an affront to our youthful desire and vision for the church. Some view a congregation filled with many older adults as a dying church.

Declining memberships, dwindling finances, and efforts to reach a new generation may consume church leaders, so that learning to appreciate the unique challenges and gifts of aging get in the way of emphasizing intentional ministry by, with, and for senior adults. In addition, the emphasis in many churches on children, youth, and young families makes it difficult for us to appreciate the significance of older adults. Older adults may come to believe, rightly or wrongly, that their congregation no longer values their wisdom, faith, experience, or knowledge. With so much emphasis on young people, older adults may believe that their faith needs no longer matter. As a result, it is important to identify some of the many reasons why congregations *should* reach out to older adults and create opportunities for intentional senior-adult ministry.

In the mid-1990s, while I was serving as the director of older-adult ministries at the General Board of Discipleship (now Discipleship Ministries) of The United Methodist Church, I had a visit from a bishop of my denomination. I had just completed my first book, *Aging: God's Challenge to Church and Synagogue,* which was co-written with my friend and mentor, the late Rev. Dr. Donald Clingan. I was filled with enthusiasm and joy at the many possibilities for helping church leaders create ministry by, with, and for older adults. The bishop, however, was not.

On that particular day, I was faced with one of my greatest challenges in my ministry. The bishop said quite straightforwardly that he was not interested in ministry with older adults. In fact, he went on to say, that neither the church, the bishops, nor my own agency had any real interest or investment in ministry with older adults. The church was declining in membership, and the need was to reach young people for Christ, not worry about older adults. I was in shock and silence. I had been naïve enough to believe that with an aging population, the church would be as enthusiastic as I was to engage in intentional ministries by, with, and for older adults.

After the bishop left my office, I prayed. I asked God if I should leave my position with the General Board of

Discipleship as the director of older-adult ministries and return to my annual conference and again assume the role as a church pastor. And I prayed for a long time.

Eventually, through prayer and with the support and encouragement of my colleagues from other denominations, I again felt that God had called me to this particular ministry on behalf of older adults in The United Methodist Church. I had been equipped for this ministry by years of training and education and through years of practice in the local church and in other settings. God called, and I accepted. Even if the church was not ready or particularly interested in ministry with older adults, I believe it was God's will for me to stand firm in my faith and in my convictions on behalf of older adults. Over the years, it became my goal, my vocation, my passion, to help the church fully understand the need for this vital ministry in our aging world and to see this ministry as an opportunity. My goal in ministry has been to equip and train church leaders, both clergy and laity, with the knowledge, tools, vision, and resources for intentional ministry by, with, and for older adults.

There are several important reasons why churches should engage in intentional ministry by, with, and for senior adults:

There are more older adults in the United States population.

As a result of medical/dental advances, scientific discoveries, job safety, lifestyle choices, and a host of other variables, more people are living longer lives than ever before. Projections indicate that the older population will continue to grow significantly in the future. In 1900 there were 3.1 million people in the United States age sixty-five and older. Today, there are more than 47.8 million, and by 2060, there will be 98 million people in the U.S. who are sixty-five years of age and older. People age sixty-five and older represented 14.9 percent of the population in 2015, but are expected to grow to be 21.7 percent of the population by 2040.[2]

Since 1900, the percentage of Americans 65 years and older has more than tripled (from 4.1 percent in 1900 to 14.9 percent in 2015), and the number has increased over fifteen times (from 3.1 million to 47.8 million). In 2015, people reaching age 65 have an average life expectancy of an additional 19.4 years (20.6 years for females and 18 years for males).[3]

Our aging population is a result of at least three significant developments: lower birth rates, a decline in infant mortality rates, and more people living to old age. The prolongation of average life expectancy and the decrease in the birth rates have given rise to an unprecedented demographic transition with the aging of America. Today, people can expect to live twenty to thirty or more years beyond the normal retirement age.

Older adults make up a significant percentage of the membership of many congregations.

As a result of an aging population, many congregations are seeing increasing numbers of older members. This is true in rural and urban areas. With fewer children and youth, and with more people living to old age, older adults may make up a significant percentage of a congregation's membership. Although not all older adults claim to have a strong religious faith, older adults are generally more religious than other age groups, and they make up a large proportion of the people sitting in church pews.

While The United Methodist Church does not keep statistical records on the age of members, estimates from various sources indicate that nearly two-thirds of our membership is made up of adults fifty years of age and older, while one-third is sixty-five years of age and older. In almost any church, older adults make up a large proportion of total church membership. They are present when the church doors are open, and they provide leadership, service, and financial resources to the church. The church is blessed, indeed, that it has a number of older people actively engaged in its total ministry.

But we must also remember that there are many older adults in our communities who have never had a vital relationship with God or participated in the life of any church. They may have been raised in families that had no time or concern for religion. Or the busyness of life, with work, career, and raising a family may have made it easy to ignore church attendance. Whatever the cause, there are multitudes of older adults who are facing the final years of their life without the secure strength of the Christian faith, the companionship of others, and the opportunity to express themselves in ministry and service.

A question for pastors and other church leaders might be, "How long has it been since your church received a seventy-year-old into membership on profession of faith?" There should be some people this age and older coming into membership every year, for there are many who need to experience a growing, loving relationship with God through Jesus Christ, the fellowship of other believers, and the opportunity to find meaning and purpose through service.

Perhaps the most disconcerting reality about our graying congregations is not that our population is aging but that many churches have done virtually nothing, or, at best, very little, to understand or to prepare for this change in age demographics. With growing numbers of older adults in our pews, congregations have an opportunity to be blessed by the gifts, prayers, presence, service, and witness of their older members. A church for all ages is a multigenerational congregation committed to creating the conditions of life able to fulfill the great potential that older people still have. The church needs to understand that this is an age of opportunity and that the church must begin to take seriously the spiritual needs of older adults and help them grow in Christian maturity. The challenges and transitions people experience as they grow older should not be overlooked or undervalued by the church.

Aging is changing.

Today people who are sixty-five and older are generally healthier, wealthier, and more active than were previous generations of older adults. We must replace stereotypes of aging as decline, disease, dependency, and dementia with empowering views of aging such as independence, activity, well-being, and service.

Medical advances in the prevention of and treatment of acute infections, increased emphasis on health and fitness, sensible changes in lifestyles, such as ceasing to smoke, decreasing use of alcohol, and eating a well-balanced diet, mean that our bodies will, in all likelihood, still be in good shape by the time we reach old age. Because of these factors and many others, older adults today differ from their counterparts of even a generation ago. As a group, they are better educated, healthier, and better protected by public and private services.

In many ways, we are living in an age paradox: People tend to stay younger longer *and* older longer. Youth and young adulthood have stretched over a longer period of years. Instead of young adulthood ending by the time people reach the age of thirty, during the past recent decades, young adulthood has stretched well into the thirties. Young people are delaying marriage, but most still eventually tie the knot. In the 1970s, eight in ten people married by the time they turned thirty. Today, not until the age of forty-five have eight in ten people married. Also, more young people today live in their parents' home than in any other arrangement: one in three young people, or about 24 million eighteen- to thirty-four-year olds, lived in their parents' home in 2015 (Census Bureau, "The Changing Economics and Demographics of Young Adulthood From 1975–2016").[4]

Ageism

Ageism is prevalent in our culture, and older adults are frequently stereotyped as dull, weak, and unproductive. Ageism affects every element of society—from our feelings about our appearance to expectations about work and retirement. Ageism, which can be defined as the systematic stereotyping and discrimination against people because they are old, is a cultural phenomenon whose acceptance is long-standing. Ageist attitudes are perpetuated in many ways, from birthday cards that belittle growing older to the lack of positive images of older adults in the media and the widespread use of demeaning language about old age, such as "greedy geezer," "old hag," or "dirty old man."

Institutions also perpetuate ageism. Corporations and businesses often reinforce ageist stereotypes by not hiring or promoting older workers or by changing the job descriptions so that older workers are categorically unqualified or overqualified. Even our health-care system focuses on acute care and cure rather than chronic care, which most older adults need. In addition, government policies often reflect a negative view of older workers by negating the value of Social Security and Medicare to the financial well-being of older people. The government calls these programs "entitlements" rather than social programs that were paid for by workers.

Ageism is manifested in society's worship of youth and in our own anxiety over wrinkles and gray hair. How we age often depends on the way we internalize the images of growing old.

Positive images of aging in our society are often lacking, thus growing older is viewed as something to be denied, avoided, and hidden. Because of the stereotypes associated with being older, many people refuse to see themselves as older adults and want nothing to do with older-adult programs. They perpetuate the myth that aging is the problem. Aging isn't the problem; *ageism* in our society is the problem.

Unfortunately, ageism is widespread not only in society, but also in the church. The image of an older congregation is seen as outdated and closed-minded, one that holds steadfastly to tradition, is a hindrance to church growth, an affront to the "youthful" desire and vision of the church, or one that is simply dying.

Ageism in our youth-oriented culture makes it difficult for us to appreciate the significance of growing old. Ageism in our churches is often compounded by the negative stereotypes that many older adults hold about themselves. Ageist thinking leads older adults to believe that they should "step aside" at church. As a result, older adults may not take full advantage of opportunities presented to them because of self-imposed ageism.

Ageism can cause congregations to neglect the spiritual and emotional needs of older adults. This is especially true if church leaders do not listen to the needs of older adults, but assume they know what older adults need.

Ageism is the perfect target for congregational advocacy because it affects everyone. We can undermine ageism when people of all ages reject our culture's ageist intentions. The vital task for people of all ages, both young and old alike, is to come to grips with our own internalized ageism, the voices that whisper "too old" or "too young," that make people victims of their own marginalization. At times, there may be good reasons to disengage from some activity, but age alone is not reason enough. Church leaders must encourage and empower older adults for continued involvement in the life of the congregation. If ministry to an aging population is viewed as a strength and an opportunity, then we will be able to affirm and use the gifts and graces of older adults and develop intentional ministry with senior adults. However, if older adults are regarded as a liability whose productive years are behind them, then congregational life and ministry will reflect those attitudes.

Living longer offers other challenges.

The longer people live, the more likely they are to experience many challenges, including health and financial challenges. The "golden years" are not always bright and uplifting for older adults, and the process of aging is not always positive. Aging is also about physical decline, lost relationships, and loss of roles, income, and housing. Older adults may face managing their own or a spouse's chronic health conditions. They may also experience grief caused by the death of loved ones, limitations in mobility, and increasing dependence.

It is helpful to remember that aging is a natural process that includes both gains and losses. Everyone ages differently. There are no two older adults who are exactly alike. Through the years, people with different genetic backgrounds, having different life experiences, age in many and various ways. As a result, older adults are perhaps the least homogeneous group of any age-cohort. Every older adult has had different social, educational, physical, biological, emotional, and religious experiences over the years.

How we age is affected by several factors: lifestyle, exercise, nutrition, stress, and a variety of others. Heredity is another important factor, particularly in defining characteristics of our physical appearance as we grow older, such as balding or graying hair.

Congregations are often composed of older adults who are experiencing both the positive attributes of aging as well as its challenges. Older adults want to serve and feel useful and needed. They want to be in a growing relationship with God and others. They want to feel safe, respected, and loved. As they age, their life challenges may become magnified. We need to embrace the changes in aging and support the independence and dignity of older people.

The search for meaning and purpose as we grow older

Historically, older adults were valued because they had useful skills. They could play important roles as carriers of knowledge and tradition. In modern times, older adults are often devalued by a culture that emphasizes a person's worth based on self-reliance, work, and productivity. Today, as traditions cease to play an important role and knowledge becomes the domain of experts and technology, aging people tend to become marginalized, even in our churches.

Growing older is a season in search of a purpose. As more and more people are living into old age, questions related to meaning and purpose take on greater importance. One reason for this concern is that old age can be isolating and depressing for many people. This may be due to physical circumstances, financial constraints, cognitive problems, or multiple chronic health conditions and disability. Work comes to an end, children grow up and leave home, marriage relationships change, friends move away, a spouse becomes ill or dies, community and social activities may be curtailed, and health deteriorates. All this affects meaning and purpose as we grow older.

As previously indicated, well-being involves more than good physical health, financial security, and social support; well-being also involves having meaning and purpose in life. Often feeling that they have outlived their usefulness, many older adults struggle to find meaning and purpose. Older adults tend to give up on life prematurely when their environment offers few opportunities for continued growth and stimulation. It becomes too easy for older adults to feel that they are worthless or have no meaning if they do not see themselves as being created in the very image of God, a fact that no amount of productivity or nonproductivity can change.

Intentional ministry with older adults involves congregations helping adults find meaning and purpose in the later years. Helping older adults to continue learning and using their skills, expertise, and knowledge can enrich not only the life of the older person but can provide exceptional benefits for the whole community and all ages.

Need for spiritual growth and faithful aging in the later years

The late Bette Davis is often quoted as saying, "Old age is no place for sissies." Some older adults live in a world of fear and denial. They fear the coming of old age with its advancing frailty and cognitive decline; they worry about being a burden on their family and others; and they fear outliving their financial resources. The struggles and fears that often come with age can challenge even the most faithful Christians.

For some older adults, religious change and different styles of worship and music can be bewildering. Older adults may feel isolated within their own place of worship and at odds with the pastoral staff and other church leaders. Indifference to their spiritual needs will not help older adults grow in faith and spiritual maturity as they age. Older adults who are homebound or who reside in nursing homes or assisted living facilities also need the presence of familiar religious symbols, hymns, and rituals to support their continuing identity as members of the church. Placing a greater emphasis on the faith development of children and youth while ignoring or devaluing the spiritual well-being of midlife and older adults is an unfortunate undertaking for churches, and it ultimately hinders the faith formation of people of all ages.

While the church's attention and commitment to older adults should always be evident in the life of the congregation, it has to be recognized that the growth in numbers of older adults invites congregations to new forms and methods in helping older adults grow in faith. Congregations can make this an age of opportunity by helping older adults express and witness their faith and share their wisdom with succeeding generations. Empowering older adults in their faithful aging means that older adults can know and trust God throughout their later years. It involves older adults with the will and knowledge to help build the body of Christ and to serve the needs of the community.

God loves older adults.

In Leviticus 19:32 (NIV), God commands us to *"stand up in the presence of the aged, show respect for the elderly and revere your God."*[5] Because society and many of our churches focus so intently on youth, it is often difficult for older adults to know and remember that God loves them. When churches emphasize ministry with young people and fail to recognize the needs of an aging congregation, older adults may feel that even God has no time for them. Of course, God loves all humankind, regardless of age or station in life. *"God's steadfast love endures forever, and God's faithfulness to all generations" (Psalm100:5).* An important role for the church is to help older adults know that no matter what they may be experiencing, no matter what physical problems they have, or what cognitive issues they may face, God loves them.

In the creation story, God blesses all that God has made (Genesis 1:31). When a person reaches the age of sixty-five, our faith teaches us that God does not take away God's blessing. In fact, the Scriptures are quite clear that God often uses older adults for God's purpose and mission. Abraham is seventy-five years old when he is commanded by God to leave his home (Genesis 12:1-4). Moses is eighty years old when he speaks to Pharaoh after God appears to him in the form of a burning bush (Exodus 3:1-12 and 7:1-7).

God's love for all people is creative and unconditional. People have dignity and worth, not because they have achieved some measure of success or experience or the esteem of their friends and community. People are worthy in the eyes of God because they are made in God's image. Just being with older adults allows God to use us as channels for God's love.

Older adults have much to teach us. Our learning is not only about aging and the aging process, but about life and faith. And about trusting a God of mystery. In the New Testament, two older adults witness the glory of God in the birth of Jesus Christ: Simeon, who is in the temple, takes Jesus in his arms and praises God (Luke 2:25-35). Anna, a prophet, who is eighty-four years of age, at the sight of the baby Jesus, praised God and began "to speak about the child to all who were looking for the redemption of Jerusalem" (Luke 2:36-38).

In 1 Samuel 3, Eli provides us with a glimpse of inter-generational learning. The boy Samuel has never heard the voice of God. One night, God visits Samuel; but Samuel, in his youthfulness, fails to recognize that it is God calling him. Eli, who is old, teaches Samuel that the voice he hears is God. Likewise, Paul (the elder) teaches Timothy (the young man) the importance of spiritual growth and of conveying God's word to others (I Timothy 4).

The Bible suggests that long life is a gift from God. It is a reward for faithfulness. As the writer of Proverbs says, "Gray hair is a crown of glory; it is gained in a righteous life

(Proverbs 16:31). Wisdom, which is also a gift from God, can be with older adults: "Is wisdom with the aged, and understanding in length of days?" (Job 12:12) and "The glory of youths is their strength, but the beauty of the aged is their gray hair" (Proverbs 20:29).

The Bible is realistic in conveying the hardships of aging and old age, but it also proclaims the blessings associated with growing old. In the span of many centuries covered by the Bible, it should be no surprise that different perspectives on age and aging appear.

> *"Do not cast me off in the time of old age; do not forsake me when my strength is spent"* (Psalm 71:9).

> *"So even to old age and gray hairs, O God, do not forsake me, until I proclaim your might to all the generations to come"* (Psalm 71:18).

> *"Listen to your father who begot you, and do not despise your mother when she is old"* (Proverbs 23:22).

> *"Listen to me, O house of Jacob. . . . even to your old age I am he, even when you turn gray I will carry you. I have made, and I will bear; I will carry and will save"* (Isaiah 46:3a, 4).

On occasion, Jesus was confronted with issues that involved aging. Once Nicodemus came to him and asked, "How can anyone be born after having grown old? Can one enter a second time into the mother's womb and be born?"

(John 3:4). Another time, Jesus reveals the kind of death Peter will experience when he gets old:

> *"Very truly, I tell you, when you were younger, you used to fasten your own belt and to go wherever you wished. But when you grow old, you will stretch out your hands, and someone else will fasten a belt around and take you where you do not wish to go"* (John 21:18).

As a church, we emphasize the priesthood of all believers, not the superiority of any particular leadership role or age group. There are many wonderful passages of Scripture concerning the blessings associated with aging and old age:

> *"I have been young, and now am old, yet I have not seen the righteous forsaken or their children begging bread"* (Psalm 37:25).

> *"For old age is not honored for length of time, or measured by number of years; but understanding is gray hair for anyone and a blameless life is ripe old age"* (Wisdom of Solomon 4:8-9, Apocrypha).

Although the Judeo-Christian tradition rejects what some religious cultures call ancestor worship, the Bible does place great importance on children honoring their parents:

> *"Honor your father and your mother, so that your days may be long in the land that the Lord your God is giving you"* (Exodus 20:12).

> *"My child, help you father in his old age, and do not grieve him as long as he lives; even if his mind fails, be patient with him; because you have all your faculties do not despise him"* (Sirach 3:12-13, Apocrypha).

> *"Do not speak harshly to an older man, but speak to him as to a father . . . to older women as mothers"* (I Timothy 5:1-2).

With the many wonderful Scripture passages listed above, we gain both understanding and insight into the nature of God and God's love for aging people. It is clear from Scripture that God loves older adults.

The future of the church is in the hands of older adults.

We often hear that young people are the future of the church; however, in reality, the future of the church is in the hands of older adults. Older adults play an increasingly vital role in the future of the church.

First, older adults, who represent a large proportion of church membership, as a group give proportionately more financially to the church. They help to pay the bills and provide for ministry. They give financially to children's and youth ministries, to scouting programs, and to mission endeavors. And, in many congregations, the older adults are the ones who are keeping the church doors open.

Second, older adults provide leadership in the church. They are the leaders and teachers in the congregation, proclaiming and teaching the Christian faith. They are preaching the Word of God, teaching the Scriptures, and telling the stories. They are demonstrating Christ's love as mentors, teachers, and leaders. They are teaching and learning from children and youth. They are inspiring and being energized by young people. They are caring for the sick, frail, and needy. They are making God real through living their faith as leaders and teachers.

Third, older adults are present and active in the life of the church. They participate in adult Bible study, Sunday school classes, women's and men's fellowship and study groups. They are present in worship and engage in spiritual growth opportunities. Older adults are often the first to sign up, the first to attend, the first to invite, the first to welcome, and the last to leave.

Fourth, older adults are engaged in service. They want to feel useful. They need to be needed. Older adults want to experience meaning and purpose in their lives. They want to make a significant difference in the lives of others. Older adults have time, and they have practical knowledge gained from years of experience. Churches that invite, equip, and empower older adults for service are making a difference in the lives of older adults and in the communities they serve.

Conclusion

The myths related to aging would have us conclude that all older adults are economically disadvantaged and physically frail. There is a general belief that older people are ready to disengage from society and are content to sit at home alone, waiting for death to release them from the confines of their misery. In the past, this view provided churches with the following two options for ministry: (1) ignore older adults, while emphasizing the faith and spiritual needs of children, youth, and families; or (2) provide only ministry *to* and *for* older adults. Meaningful ministry *by* and *with* older adults was not envisioned because of ageism and lack of understanding on the part of church leaders. The church viewed older adults through a rather narrow lens, believing that nothing much happened in the lives of older adults, that they already enjoyed spiritual well-being because of their church membership and advanced age, and that they wanted to be left alone.

When we are caught up in the ageism of our culture, we fail to see that the majority of older adults are healthy, active, and involved in life. Although many older adults experience the effects of chronic health conditions, they often report that their health is good to excellent. Older adults are involved in the world around them. They seek out new opportunities for learning and are mentors for succeeding generations. They want to make a difference in the life of their family, community, church, and world. Churches that break free from the paralyzing grip of ageism will find an avenue for exciting and challenging ministry. They will see this as an age of opportunity for the church and for older adults themselves.

Intentional ministry by, with, and for boomers and other older adults invites us to come to grips with our own feelings about aging and growing old. Intentional ministry with older adults means that we are willing to grapple with our own attitudes and feelings about aging and old age. Unless we see ourselves in the older adults around us, we may never accept the fact that we will someday be old ourselves. Getting past the wrinkles and seeing the souls of older adults is necessary for authentic and faithful ministry.

As we engage in ministry with older people, we not only learn what older people are like (uniquely created and different from one another), but we also learn something about ourselves. Many people think of becoming old as becoming a problem. We may even associate old age with death. Because we fear death, we fear old age. As a result, we fear contact with older adults because they show us our own futures.

Another reason many church leaders fail to recognize the importance and value of intentional older-adult ministry is because they have had little or no training in gerontology (the study of aging) or older-adult ministry and have little understanding of the aging process and the needs and challenges of older adults. God calls the church in this age of opportunity to a new responsibility in intentional ministry by, with, and for older adults.

CHAPTER 2

Understanding the Aging Process

"Gray hair is a crown of glory; it is gained in a righteous life."

—PROVERBS 16:31

The Bible teaches that long life is a blessing. Most of us would like to have a long, full, and active life, but few us want to age and grow old. There are many theories about why we age; aging in humans (and animals) can be seen as either an inevitable process of wear and tear, or as an inherent biological process by which the lifespan of each species is more or less predetermined. Many people are familiar with the verse from Psalm 90:10: "The days of our life are seventy years, or perhaps eighty, if we are strong" (the threescore and ten found in the King James Version). But, in Genesis 6:3, we also read, "Then the Lord said, 'My spirit shall not abide in mortals forever, for they are flesh; their days shall be one hundred twenty years.'"

In some ways, human life can be viewed through the lens of three ages. The first age, from birth to about thirty years, is a time of **acquiring**. Young people are learning and growing. They are being schooled and equipped for adulthood. The second age, from thirty to about sixty years, is a time of **doing**. Adults are working and pursuing career goals, marrying, and raising families. The third age, from sixty to ninety years or death, is a time of **being**. Older adults, having accumulated a lifetime of acquiring and doing in the first two ages of life, now have the opportunity to age more fully with the gifts of wisdom, knowledge, and experience. Generativity and wisdom are the hallmarks of the third age.

All three ages of human life are vital and important for the fulfillment of humanity. However, some people who do not grow to a "ripe old age" may also experience all three ages during a shorter lifespan.

The third age is specifically designed by God to bring older adults ever closer to a loving relationship with God and to their true selves. And although our culture declares that doing (and being productive) is the most important task, I disagree. We are not called "human doings"; we are called "human beings." The greatest task is the fulfillment of the third age.

When we think about older people, many descriptors come to mind. Older adults can be healthy and active, transitionally impaired, homebound, frail, or dying. They may be married, divorced, widowed, remarried, or always single. They may be providing care for an aging parent, spouse, adult dependent child, or neighbor. They may be retired, working full- or part-time, raising a grandchild, volunteering with a community agency, or serving in a leadership role in church. They may live in their own home or with another relative, in an assisted living facility, nursing home, or in co-housing. Even the above descriptors do not cover all the possibilities of aging and older adulthood.

However, keeping the above in mind, these are some of the people—the older adults—for whom the church must be engaged in intentional ministry. They have needs, longings, desires, and challenges. Their spiritual growth as Christians should be of particular concern to the church. They need the church and its fellowship, and they need to experience a loving relationship with God through Jesus Christ.

Engaging in new directions in senior-adult ministry means that church leaders must seek to understand older adults as people. Many of us have been operating under the influence of misconceptions about old age and what happens when people grow older. Stereotypes commonly accepted about aging and senior adults must be examined and, when proven erroneous, discarded.

Sometimes later life is defined as chronological age, functional age, and subjective age. Chronological age is the number of years a person has lived. Functional age refers to what a person is physically or cognitively able to do. Subjective age refers to how old a person actually feels (*and some days are better than others!*).

Classifying a person as "old" depends on whom you ask and what you measure. The simplest index is chronological age, but that is not a satisfactory measure in individual cases. Aging is a continuum that is not easily divided into clear and concise segments. The body does not age uniformly. A person may have a "young" cardiovascular system and an "old" digestive system. We can each think of people who are "old" or "young" for their age. It all depends on how people go through the aging process.

In the past, becoming a grandparent was thought of as the beginning of older adulthood. Today, many people resist the idea of being an "older adult" at sixty-five (this is especially true for baby boomers). People still see themselves as being active and involved, learning and creating, and engaging fully with their family, community, and the world. "They're not older adults," they say. Perhaps it is helpful to keep in mind that chronological age is a relatively meaningless variable. Chronological age is only a way of marking human events and experiences, such as beginning to receive Social Security or Medicare, or receiving *senior discounts* at restaurants or the theater.

Phases of Retirement

Retirement is a unique stage of life in our modern society, but it is not easy to define. People don't stop living because they have retired from a particular job or career. Many people *keep on keeping on* even after they have retired, especially if their health is still good. They may be working part- or full-time, engaged in volunteer work, or heading back to college to finish a degree. We'll look at retirement a bit more fully later in this chapter. However, as we consider the need for intentional ministry by, with, and for older adults, we will consider retirement in three phases: Active Phase (Go-Goes), Passive Phase (Slow-Goes), and Final Phase (No-Goes).

Go-Goes are in the active phase of retirement. During the active phase of retirement, older adults are often pursuing a variety of interests. They are not sitting in a rocking chair waiting for death to come. Although they may be retired from work, they may be starting a new career or working part time. During the active phase of retirement, they may be volunteering in a school or hospital or serving Meals on Wheels. They are traveling, caregiving, grandparenting, and taking advantage of learning opportunities. When the church starts a new worship service, Bible study, or plans a retreat or trip, they are present, supportive, and providing leadership. They are active and engaged in ministry as well as in life.

Slow-Goes are in the passive phase. During the passive phase of retirement, older adults are beginning to slow down. Their energy and health begin to ebb, and extensive travel is replaced with shorter visits to family and friends. They may even experience depression and frustration because they can't do what they once did. Or they may be the primary caregivers for a spouse or partner or raising a grandchild or grandchildren and be unable to participate as actively or as fully as they would like. Their health as caregivers may be the cause for this passive phase. As primary caregivers, they may not be able to attend worship or other church functions unless respite care is provided for their loved ones. In any event, they are slowing down, either as a result of their own health or as a result of caring for others.

No-Goes are in the final phase. During the final phase of retirement, health problems restrict mobility; frailty increases; and end-of-life concerns take on a new and different urgency. Home health-care services or alternative housing may be sought. Needing to vacate a home after many years and move into the home of an adult child or a nursing home because of physical or cognitive limitations reminds the older person that life is growing short. Visitation by the pastor and/or laity and parish nurse ministry becomes increasingly important for older adults during the final phase of retirement.

Life Changes in Later Maturity

Aging is not a disease, and old age is not an illness. Aging is a natural process of development that includes both losses and gains. However, there are certain experiences commonly found in later maturity such as physical changes, work and retirement changes, family-life changes, and financial changes.

Physical Changes

Although aging is most commonly associated with growing older, we must keep in mind that the aging process begins from the moment of birth and brings changes in the physical makeup of each person throughout life. As we grow older, certain physical changes affect many senior adults: gray hair; wrinkling of skin; changes in reproductive capacity, immune system response, and cardiovascular functioning. The bodies we had at forty are different from those we have at seventy.

Of all the physical changes associated with growing older, people are more acutely aware of the cosmetic changes. Thinning, gray hair, pronounced wrinkles, and narrowing shoulders all come with advancing age. Within our culture, these changes are not greeted with enthusiasm because, in a society that seems to cherish youth, these changes make people look old.

We know that lifestyle choices, environmental factors, nutrition, and health maintenance can influence the optimum functioning and appearance of our bodies. Everyone experiences the aging process differently; no two people age at the same rate or in the same way. Also, some organ systems within our own bodies age at different rates.

Physical changes involve sensory changes. The five sensory organs—eyes, ears, nose, tongue, skin—are each affected to some degree as people age. Gradual changes in vision include decreased visual acuity and depth perception; decreased ability to discriminate between colors; increased sensitivity to glare; a harder time seeing things that are near (increased farsightedness or presbyopia), which is one reason churches should have large-print hymnals and bulletins; and the need for stronger light. As we age, hearing, too, gradually diminishes, especially for higher frequencies.

Decreasing perception in the senses of smell and taste is common. The ability to perceive all four taste qualities (sweet, salty, sour, and bitter) diminishes as people age. And because of thinning skin and the loss of elasticity of the layers of the skin, people have difficulty feeling the sensations of hot or cold, and people bruise more easily.

Muscle strength and flexibility also decrease with age. People may begin to walk more slowly or have difficulty coordinating the steps up the stairs. And, as we age, our skeletal system changes; we get shorter. On average, we lose two inches in height between the ages of twenty and seventy because our bones thin and shrink in the spinal column and in the arms and legs.

While these physical and sensory changes occur in all people as they age, the degree in which they affect individuals varies greatly. The key is how we take care of ourselves. Keeping active and healthy throughout life can result in an old age that is productive and rewarding.

It was once the view that when people reached retirement age, all their time would be spent managing their health. This was sometimes thought of as the "rocking chair" lifestyle. People rested from their labor, sat in their rocking chairs, dealt with their failing health, and died within six months to two years following retirement. Today, as a result of medical advances and changes in lifestyles, people at retirement can live without fear or great worry of impending death. Aging and retirement are no longer synonymous with death.

With better health, even the gender gap in the United States is substantially changing. Women live longer than men in the United States and in nearly every country in the world. But in the United States and in many other developed countries, the gender gap is narrowing, resulting in an increasing number of men, relative to women, surviving to old age.

"In 1990, there was a seven-year gap in the life expectancy between men and women. By 2013, this gap had narrowed to less than five years. It is not that women are dying sooner, but that men's life expectancy is increasing at a faster pace . . . If the current trends continue, men's life expectancy could approach that of women within the next few decades." (Population Bulletin, Vol. 70, No. 2, December 2015, 13)[1]

The typical person reaching the age of sixty-five can likely look forward to many more years of a healthy, disability free-life. Older adults can continue to be contributing members of society and church.

Work and Retirement Changes

Another consideration for being an "older adult" has been retirement. Although retirement is a relatively modern phenomenon, the age of sixty-five has traditionally been thought of as the time of retirement.

Some scholars attribute the choice of sixty-five as the age for retirement to the Old Age and Survivors Pension Act that Otto Von Bismarck pushed through as the first chancellor of the German Empire in 1889. The United States followed in 1935 with its own Social Security program. Although the original Social Security Act of 1935 was not involved in establishing a compulsory retirement age, the choice of age sixty-five seems to have carried over from Social Security to mandatory retirement policies.

By age sixty-five, retired workers were now considered to be older adults. The work day was idle, and life had to be purposely filled with other activity. However, traditional retirement is being reimagined as many older adults continue working in the later years. "The U.S. labor force is growing older. In 2014, adults ages fifty-five and older made up about 22 percent of the labor force, up from 12 percent in 1990. By 2022, their share is projected to increase to 26 percent."[2] That means that more than one out of four older adults will still be working and in the labor force.

There are many reasons for this change in behavior related to retirement. Recessions can affect retirement expectations by putting pressure on older workers to stay on the job. The Great Recession (2007 to 2009) certainly contributed to the rise in older adults remaining in the workforce. Savings, incomes, and home values of many older adults were dramatically affected, with shrinking nest eggs, large amounts of debt, and little or no personal savings. But, there are many other factors as well. In recent years, employer pensions and medical benefits for retirees have largely been replaced by employee-funded *defined contribution plans*, such as 401(k)s. The uncertainties of 401(k)s may cause many adults near or at retirement age to reconsider leaving the workplace.

Mandatory retirement ages have been abolished for older adults in many industries, clearing the way for employees to work beyond the age of sixty or sixty-five (although there is still a mandatory retirement age for clergy in The United Methodist Church). The age at which workers can receive full Social Security benefits has increased from sixty-five to sixty-six to sixty-seven for those born after 1942. In addition, the tax penalty for earning an income while receiving Social Security benefits has been reduced. With older adults in better health and living longer, it is possible for them to work into older ages.

There are many reasons people retire, perhaps almost as many reasons as there are retirees. Some of the most often cited reasons for retirement are: affordability of retirement, lack of job satisfaction, feeling "pushed out" by an employer, the desire for more personal and leisure time, and health status (of self, spouse or partner, or aging parents).

It is also helpful to remember that, in most cases, work is not as physical as it was in the past. With good health, people are able to work for more years. In addition to financial considerations for continuing to work, people stay in the workforce because of ongoing career interests, wanting to stay productive, and finding meaning in work. While some older workers will stay on the job, others will temporarily leave the workforce and then reenter it. Many older adults will retire, rest up, and essentially get ready for a new phase of life. They will pursue learning opportunities, launch a new career or start a business, or contribute to their communities through volunteerism and civic engagement. Retirement is becoming a transition, rather than a destination. For many older adults, true retirement may get deferred until much later in life.

Despite the desire and/or need to work in retirement, many older adults may not be able to do so because of health concerns, family caregiving needs, age discrimination in the workplace, or changes in the work environment or job description. For people whose life was wrapped up in their daily work, who lived for their jobs or careers, actual retirement may seem like a kind of death. Some employees are fortunate enough to work for companies that allow for flextime schedules that allow older workers to ease into retirement by replacing full-time work with a part-time schedule.

As a result of many jobs going overseas, new technology, robotics, and other workplace changes, older workers may find their career jobs disappearing before they are ready to retire, requiring them to seek "bridge jobs." Bridge jobs often provide workers with a different type of job or employment that will carry them over between a career job and full retirement, often with lower pay and fewer benefits.

A widely held view of retirement is that retirement has an adverse effect on health and leads to an early death. We've all heard stories about a retiree who carefully plans for retirement, only to become sick and die within a brief period of time following retirement. One problem with such stories is that they are never clear about the health status of the retiree before retirement. Retired people are no more likely to be sick than are people of the same age who are still working. In fact, for some older adults who worked in harsh environments and in high-risk and stressful occupations, retirement may actually provide improvements in health.

At any rate, retirement does bring with it many changes. Regular pay is stopped; there may be a pension check, but it is probably not as large as the workday wage. Contact with colleagues and fellow workers is cut off except on special occasions or through social media. The feeling of usefulness to do one's best to achieve some degree of success or advancement is lost. People may wonder "now that I am no longer in the workplace and retired, or no longer raising or nurturing a family, 'who am I?' Retirees have more time than before and may not know how to use it. Since many retirement years are expected to be healthy, active years, there is a growing concern about what people can, should, and will do after they retire from paid employment.

Attitudes regarding employment and retirement may be critical to deciding how individuals allocate this time, and their attitudes directly determine how they adjust. Finances, health, and physical mobility, relationships, and social involvement are key factors in how well people adjust to retirement. In addition, finding meaning and a new sense of purpose in the later years, which can be quite difficult for some older adults, is another important factor to retirement adjustment. Churches that are intentional in ministry by, with, and for senior adults can assist older adults in helping them find meaning and purpose in their later years. Churches can also play an important role in helping retirees replace their work networks with new social networks through small-group ministries, men's and women's fellowship groups, and Sunday school classes.

Perhaps the most difficult thing for couples to face in retirement is the illness or death of a spouse, especially if the death occurs in the early retirement years. For some couples, this event results in what has been called a "spoiled retirement." Long-cherished plans may have to be modified or even abandoned, particularly in the case of a serious illness that necessitates one spouse caring for the other. In the case of a death, retirement plans may take a completely different direction for the surviving spouse.

Family-Life Changes

As we grow older, we recognize that family life changes over time. Children grow up and marry; loved ones die; and the family system changes. Families are resilient and resourceful groups that connect us to the past and to the future. Families provide a close network of emotional and practical support that shifts over time as their members and their capacities and involvements change over the life course.

The functions the family fulfills shift in importance. But an important role for many families involves caregiving—from parents nurturing children to older adults often caring for (or in some cases, raising) grandchildren, to adult children providing some level of care for their older parents. Families supply sixty to eighty percent of the initial care for dependent seniors before turning to institutional facilities when the older adults' decline becomes too physically and emotionally draining to handle alone.

It is important to note that there is little evidence that the majority of older adults are isolated from their families. While older adults usually live separate from their children and grandchildren, they may not be alone. Generally speaking, older people live near, but not with, their children and interact with them frequently. For most older adults, the family is a source of love, continuity, emotional support, meaning, and connection throughout life.

Marital satisfaction in older age has been found to be high, although the strengths and weaknesses of a particular marriage may be more apparent. The majority of older adults live with their spouse or partner. "Over half (59%) of older noninstitutionalized persons age 65+ lived with their spouse (including partner) in 2016" *(Profile of Older Americans: 2016, p 5)*.[3] The proportion of older adults living with their spouse decreases with age, especially for women, since women live longer than men.

Relationships between parents and their adult children seem to grow closer with age, and grandchildren play an important role in the lives of many older adults. Family members are typically involved to some degree with one another's lives, providing advice and emotional support, making demands on time and loyalty, and sometimes giving or seeking assistance both across and within generations.

As our population grows older, there will be a steady increase in the number of older adults with functional and cognitive disabilities. Traditionally, older adults have relied heavily on their adult children to provide support and care when they needed assistance. This is especially true among older women, who are much more likely than older men to be living alone.

"Over half (59%) of older noninstitutionalized persons age 65+ lived with their spouse (including partner) in 2016. Approximately 15.5 million or 73% of older men and 12 million or 47% of older women, lives with their

spouse. The proportion living with their spouse decreased with age, especially for women. Only 34% of women 75+ years old lived with a spouse" (Profile of Older Americans).[4]

However, recent trends in marriage and family patterns may limit the availability of adult children who are available—or willing—to provide care for older parents in the coming years. With young adults delaying marriage, children growing up in single-parent families and "blended families" and complex living arrangements by some adult children, there may be an increase in weaker family ties with less support for aging parents. Despite the strengths and positive connotations of family bonds, not all family relationships are close and affectionate. Some family bonds may be distant after experiencing conflicts over the years.

The reality of caregiving is also more complex because of the rising number of older adults who are single or childless. Studies show that older men are much more likely to be married than older women, since women live longer than men. As a result, older men are more likely to have "built-in" caregiving by their spouse. However, for widows, widowers, divorced, separated older people, people never married, and childless couples, caregiving takes on new and different dimensions.

Certainly during later life, there is the fact of aloneness. Even if children and grandchildren live nearby, older adults will often face the reality of living alone following the death of a spouse. Even the single person who has never married and has been self-sufficient over the years may find the need to think about joining forces with someone else for satisfactory living in the later years.

Some older adults decide to find new housing. Although older adults are more stationary and less likely to change residences than other age groups, there may come a time when an older person can no longer stay in his or her home. Acquiring new living arrangements can take on a sense of urgency, particularly if the older person is dealing with a significant health issue. For some older adults, just simple home maintenance needs, such as changing a light bulb in a kitchen ceiling light, can make a difference in overall well-being. Moving in with a daughter or son, while not always desirable, may become necessary. Some older adults may need to move into an assisted living facility, a nursing home, a continuing care retirement community, or into some other form of co-housing arrangement.

Financial Changes

As already indicated, retirement changes most people's financial situations. Reliance on Social Security, savings, pension, investment income, continued employment, or help from adult children or other relatives are some of the significant financial changes that might happen with retirement.

In the past, many workers received pensions upon retirement, usually in the form of *defined benefit pension plans*. In a defined benefit pension plan, the employer controls the pension. The employer invests and controls a common fund under rules defined by the ERISA (Employee Retirement Income

Security Act of 1974). Many retirees felt some sense of financial security in retirement by receiving a company pension.

Over the past two decades, many employers have dropped defined benefit plans in favor of *defined contribution plans*, which is a retirement plan in which the worker, the employer, or both contribute to a fund held by an independent financial entity. This shift in pension coverage means that older adults face more unpredictability about their income after they retire. The employee bears the brunt of the burden of the ups and downs of the stock market or other investment vehicle.

Traditional retirement financial security was likened to a "three-legged stool": Social Security, pension, and personal savings. With the advent of defined contribution plans, instead of a three-legged stool, the image most often used is the "four pillars of economic security": Social Security, pension/savings, earnings from employment (full- or part-time), and health insurance coverage (Medicare and supplemental health insurance).

Retirement is not the only financial challenge that's likely to affect older adults in our congregations today. Many older adults also have problems coping with debt, understanding their loans (especially related to reverse mortgages), and recovering from financial scams and fraud, among other issues.

Some seniors are carrying debt into retirement after years of helping children and grandchildren. The continuing high cost of health care and reductions in federal and state programs for the elderly may have an adverse effect on the financial well-being of older adults. The move to a fixed income generally makes it more difficult for retirees to cope with debt payments. Older adults who fall behind on payments may even be at risk of foreclosure and losing their homes.

Finally, the loss of a spouse can create financial challenges for the surviving wife or husband, particularly if that person was not used to managing finances. In addition, the high cost of health care prior to the death of a husband or wife and the overall funeral expenses may now add a greater financial burden for the surviving spouse.

Conclusion

There probably has never been a "golden age," when older adults enjoyed perpetual good health, never worried about finances, and were guaranteed the unquestioned respect and loving care of families. The idea of old age being the "golden years" for seniors has largely been a myth.

Although the twenty-first century is certainly no golden age, we are living in a good period for most older adults. For all its failings, medical science has assured us of long and productive lives. Better education, financial security, and the simple fact that older adults are increasingly important in our churches and communities, assure them a firm voice and respected position.

An older adult's ability to age successfully involves not only having good genes but also good attitude and coping skills. How older adults adapt to changes in life—including functional and cognitive changes, socioeconomic conditions, and even how society and the church values or devalues aging individuals—is central to successful aging.

If older adults are living longer, healthier lives, what is the purpose of living to old age? Why has God given us longer life?

Ultimately, aging is a personal matter. How aging is done depends on who is doing it. Each older person must find the answer to this question. Although there is no secret to success in aging well, advice can help. Faith and the church can help in the decision-making process; however, each older person must find his or her own answer to the value of living a longer life. As long as there is life, there is change; and even in old age, change can be good.

For more information about the aging process and older adults, see Appendix A for a list of true or false statements related to aging and older adults. Review these statements to ascertain your knowledge about aging. By reviewing these statements, you will discover something new about aging and older adults. The answers to the true or false statements are found in Appendix B.

CHAPTER 3

Aging and the
Spiritual Journey

*"Listen to me, O house of Jacob . . . even to your
old age I am he, even when you turn gray I will
carry you. I have made, and I will bear; I will
carry and will save."*

—ISAIAH 46:3-4

The search for meaning in life addresses the need for spiritual direction and growth. Spirituality involves the process of understanding life in relationship to meaning, purpose, values, and the connection to God, to others, to the world, and to nature.

Traditionally, the words "religion" and "spiritual" meant the same thing. In more recent times, the word "religion" has come to be connected with a set of beliefs and rituals, rooted in sacred text, and is connected with the public realm of membership in religious institutions. The word "spiritual" is associated with the private realm of feelings and experiences and may transcend reason, culture, and language. It is often understood as a greater power that is outside of the self, yet intimately connected with the sense of self and all that is. For some, it is the ultimate source and provider of meaning and purpose in life.

It's all too easy to confuse the term "religion" with the much broader subject of "spirituality." For many older adults, spirituality and participation in a religious organization or faith-based community may overlap. For example, sometimes seniors do not participate in church activities due to physical limitations, financial concerns, or transportation needs, yet they maintain a rich, private spiritual life through activities such as prayer and personal devotion.

Because spirituality is concerned with the deepest dimensions of all of life and is often expressed through our questions, hopes, dreams, fears, and loves, spirituality is ultimately a search for meaning. Older adults may search for God with greater intensity than younger people as a way of seeking meaning. Younger people may be more preoccupied with identity and relationships, job, family, and making a living. Older adults have both the time and the need at this point in their lives to want to draw closer to God and to grapple with the mysteries of life.

As they cope with frailty, loss, and mortality, older adults may find their faith fundamentally shaken. Yet, continuing to develop spiritually is important to most people as they age. Spiritual maturity can be an important coping strategy in dealing with the challenges of aging. Spiritual well-being is enhanced by participation in a faith community. For many older adults, spirituality and religious practice go hand in hand. For this reason, we must not undervalue the importance of congregational worship and spiritual growth in the lives of older adults.

Unfortunately, the faith needs of older adults may be overlooked by active, growing congregations. Churches that place a premium on faith formation with young people may not see the need for equipping older adults in a growing faith. While we are called to make disciples of Jesus Christ, this doesn't mean that we seek to make disciples of children, youth, and young adults only. Older adults need to experience a new (and renewed) relationship with God through Jesus Christ and to grow in faith maturity, too. An important question for church leaders is this: "What strategies are you employing to further Christian discipleship among older adults in your community?"

Continuity is important for the well-being of older adults, and this includes their participation in church. While learning new rituals and hymns can be meaningful for older adults, it is also important to remember to include old, familiar hymns that were meaningful for older adults when they were young or new in the faith. To completely ignore singing some of the "old hymns" sends a clear message to older adults that their faith experience and their faith journey is not valued by the church today. As a result, older adults may struggle with understanding and fully accepting the changes being made to make worship "contemporary."

Every person follows a unique path of faith development. Age, experience, and cognitive development influence the expression of religious faith and level of faith maturity. Mature faith involves maximizing whatever level of faith is possible, given one's emotional and intellectual abilities. As we age, our spiritual well-being is tested and refined through a variety of experiences, such as the frequent experience of loss, illness and disability, the deaths of loved ones, and changes in social position and economic conditions. Spiritual well-being affects and is affected by the older person's physical, emotional, mental, and social-economic well-being. While the church is especially concerned about meeting spiritual needs, it cannot ignore these other realities.

Although the later years do bring more time for dwelling on God and the mysteries of life, older adults need help in their search for the deep meanings of life. The church needs to help older people discover the resources that will enhance their spiritual well-being and give them new zest for living. Spiritual well-being for older adults includes knowing that God loves older people; experiencing a church that cares about older adults as individuals and as a group; remaining a vital part of the church; serving as mentors and role models; and having support systems available.

Knowing That God Loves Older People

The church must be a fellowship of people seeking God and God's purposes, demonstrating the Christian way of life in all relationships, and strengthening one another's faith. We sing the song "Jesus Loves the Little Children," and we know that Jesus does love children; but older adults also need to know that Jesus loves them. Living in a society that devalues old age, older adults may grow to believe that God does not love them because they are old. Old age can bring doubts about God's love and the Christian faith. The church must be intentional in assisting older adults to have both a sense of life purpose and a sense of well-being in relation to God. Older adults need to know and claim God's love.

Experiencing a Church That Cares about Older Adults as Individuals and as a Group

The church must be a welcoming and inviting fellowship for people of all ages. We must be careful with the language we use in church so that it is not exclusive. While we may pride ourselves on being a "family" church, this language may mean something different for older adults and for single adults. Further, if older adults hear from the pulpit only sermon illustrations relating to the challenges and transitions of youth and young adulthood, they may have difficulty understanding how faith in daily life relates to their own struggles and challenges. While the church is concerned about reaching all generations with God's message of love and gift of salvation, the church must affirm the dignity and value of older adults in the community.

Remaining a Vital Part of the Church by Making Significant Contributions to Its Ministry

While the church needs and appreciates the financial contributions made by older adults, the church must also equip and empower older adults for living out their Christian discipleship in other significant ways, even when their health and physical strength decline. If older adults are regarded as a liability whose productive years are behind them—as is often the case in our society—congregational life and ministry will reflect these attitudes. Helping older adults recapture a vision for service is important. Enabling older adults to identify and develop their spiritual gifts is not only essential for their well-being, it is vital for both church and community.

Serving as Mentors and Role Models

Faithful aging involves opportunities for older adults to give back to future generations. This involves sharing their faith, wisdom, experience, and resources with others. There is a sense in which old age really does bring with it a wide display of understanding and empathy and diversity. A tolerance for others is often manifest in this age and faith situation, too. Sharing faith and wisdom can be of great encouragement and inspiration to youthful faith seekers and chronic doubters.

The church is also one of the few institutions where intergenerational learning and opportunities for serving can occur; yet, all too often, intentional intergenerational ministry is not being planned or carried out. As a result, younger generations are not being exposed to the faith and wisdom of older adults. And, likewise, older adults are not experiencing the energy, creativity, and enthusiasm of young people.

Having Available Support Systems

Older adults experience many changes in life. Helping older adults cope with losses and the challenges of aging is an important ministry of the church. Older people need to feel needed, and their faith is enriched through interaction with others in meaningful relationships that deal with relevant issues of their lives. Being able to share with others who may be experiencing similar losses or changes in life is meaningful for all involved in the process. Ministry that helps meet the psycho-social and spiritual needs of older adults provides a valuable service that is essential to continued growth in faith and trust in God if older adults are to age in faith.

Aging Faithfully

Today, as people live longer and often retire earlier, they may experience a new spiritual awakening. We have moved from a time not long ago when aging was seen as synonymous with senility and death, to one in which a glimpse of human potential has opened up incredible possibilities. Surely, God has some purpose for adding years to our lives.

Many adults become more involved in spirituality and religion as they age for a variety of reasons. With retirement, older adults have more time to consider their interior lives.

For older adults who are uncertain about life after death and the role of salvation, focusing on greater connection with their faith and God helps them cope with the future that is before them. As people age, losses accumulate. Many older adults need the strength that comes from faith and a spiritual connection to support them through the death of loved ones, illness, loneliness, isolation, and fear.

An important role for congregations in ministry with older adults is helping older adults grow spiritually—in other words, inviting, nurturing, and equipping older adults to age faithfully! Unfortunately, effective congregational ministries that focus on the life experiences and spiritual needs of older adults are often absent. Breaking through the myths and stereotypes of aging is important for most congregations. Whether you are an older-adult or a leader of older-adult ministries, you play an important role in helping your church develop an intentional ministry with older adults that encourages and empowers older adults to age faithfully. Faith, wisdom, and experience of older adults should not be ignored because of their age or stage in life. Aging in faith is important for people at any age, but it is particularly important for people in the third and fourth quarters of life.

So, what does "aging faithfully" mean?

To age faithfully is to see and know that all of life—at every age and stage—is a gift from a loving, creator God. In the Scriptures, we read that we have been created in the image of God. We are uniquely made and wonderfully formed by God. But God's love for us doesn't stop when we are born. "Listen to me, O house of Jacob . . . even to your old age I am he; even when you turn gray I will carry you. I have made, and I will bear; I will carry and will save" (Isaiah 46:3-4). God's love for us never ends. In the midst of losses and the challenges of life, faithful aging involves knowing that all of life is a precious gift of a loving, caring God.

To age faithfully is to trust the promises of God. While the specific nature of the promise may vary, depending upon particular needs and circumstances, the fact remains that God's grace is the source of God's promises. To aging people, the promise is God's loving presence and strength. To the suffering, the promise is God's saving presence and help. To the sick, the promise is healing and comfort. To the sinner, the promise is God's forgiveness. To the dying, the promise is eternal life. Therefore, to age faithfully is to see and know that all of life—at every age and stage—is a gift of a loving, creator God. God's gift of long life for many adults is an opportunity to deepen their relationship with God, who promises to love, forgive, bless, and sustain. With the Psalmist, people aging faithfully are able to sing: "This God—his way is perfect; the promise of the Lord proves true; he is a shield for all who take refuge in him" (Psalm 18:30).

To age faithfully is to stand against the cultural prejudice about growing old. The multibillion dollar a year "anti-aging" medical and cosmetic industries keep alive the notion that young is beautiful and old is ugly. Aging faithfully means refusing to accept this supposition. We need to be reminded that "the glory of youths is their strength, but the beauty of the aged is their gray hair" (Proverbs 20:29). Relaxing our defenses concerning our wrinkles, graying hair, and even our sagging tummies is the path toward spiritual maturity. This does not mean that we don't take proper care of our minds and bodies. However, to age faithfully means to creatively accept the many changes in our lives and to maintain a spirit that grows healthier and wiser.

To age faithfully means that we develop a new understanding of self-worth. Throughout our lives, we are taught in countless ways by our society that our worth is determined by our productivity. But as mature adults, we are able to affirm the value God places upon human life, not worth that is dependent on the amount or quality of work that a person does. We sing with the Psalmist, "I have been young, and now am old, yet I have not seen the righteous forsaken . . ." (Psalm 37:25). As children of God, we are created in God's image. If our worth is in what we own or have amassed, in time we will have neither wealth nor possessions. But as we age faithfully, we come to realize that we are and always will be valued, accepted, and loved by God.

To age faithfully is to be part of a congregation that knows that spiritual growth is possible and relevant for older adults. It is to be part of a congregation that invites and equips older adults to experience a new or renewed relationship with God. Older adults, no less than people of all ages, need to grow in faith. "The righteous flourish like the palm tree, and grow like a cedar in Lebanon. . . . In old age they still produce fruit; they are always green and full of sap" (Psalm 92:12, 14). Without a growing faith, older adults lack the resource of One who can give life meaning, purpose, and hope in times of fear, loss, and uncertainty.

Finally, to age faithfully means to practice the spiritual disciplines. First, do no harm and perform acts of mercy are the beginning of our spiritual disciplines. Attending to the faith traditions of prayer, reading the Holy Scriptures, attending and participating in worship, receiving the sacrament of Holy Communion, sharing the experiences of faith with others, and meeting the needs of others are just some of the ways older adults can experience faithful aging.

Other spiritual disciplines include practicing silence, forgiveness, generosity, guided journaling, and active listening. In addition, practicing spiritual disciplines includes honoring creation and the environment, walking the labyrinth, and seeking peace and justice. As we age faithfully, we are invited to hear and respond to the words of Micah: "With what shall I come before the Lord, and bow myself before God on high? He has told you, O mortal, what is good; and what does the Lord require of you but to do justice, and to love kindness, and to walk humbly with your God? (Micah 6:6a, 8).

Conclusion

Aging is a spiritual journey. To be on an intentional spiritual journey as we grow older is to be at peace with God. It means we have accepted the reality that we live our lives under the loving gaze of a mysterious God who is ever beyond us, deeply in love with us, and always with us.

To be on a spiritual journey as we age is to live in this world with confidence that the One who has made us, loves us, and is able to provide for us, seeks our well-being. In the spirituality of aging, older adults are living in a loving relationship with God; that provides confidence and peace in this world and hope for the world to come.

Older adults want to feel and know that God is active in their lives. If congregations focus their efforts on helping older adults grow in their spiritual lives, these older adults will participate more fully in the life of the church, as they are able.

God created men and women in God's own image and placed a value upon them that does not diminish with old age. No life lived in faith is ever wasted. Each of us has a sacred responsibility to make the most of our gift of years and to help make the world a better place. Perhaps the purpose of long life is to show that life has value in itself and to share faith, knowledge, wisdom, and love with succeeding generations. Church leaders play a vital role in helping older adults realize this spiritual journey.

CHAPTER 4

The New Seniors: Boomers?

"The glory of youths is their strength, but the beauty of the aged is their gray hair."

—Proverbs 20:29

Approximately 78 million baby boomers were born between 1946 and 1964.[1] In part because of their large numbers, boomers have transformed every age they have lived. And they are likely to change basic concepts of aging, retirement, health, religion, and politics in old age.

Many of the older people in our churches today are senior adults from the silent generation. They preceded the baby boom generation and were born between 1925 and 1945. The silent generation is a smaller generation due to the lower number of births during the Great Depression, which began in 1929, and World War II (1939 to 1945).

The oldest generation, representing relatively few older adults in our churches today, is made up of senior adults from the GI or builder generation. This generation, born between 1901 and 1924, has been called the Greatest Generation due to members' participation in World War II and their visionary leadership in the development of the infrastructure and economy of the United States. At one time, this generation made up the largest number of older adults in our congregations. They served as the leaders in our churches, both from the pulpit and in the pew. As a result of old age and death, their ranks are thinning in number.

Boomers are the largest generation reaching old age. On January 1, 2016, leading-edge boomers began turning seventy years of age. Boomers are a diverse, multifaceted, and complex generation. They are CEOs, laborers, technicians, professionals, managers, and supervisors, homemakers, retirees, and the homeless. They are learning a lot about themselves while advancing through middle age and into later life.

Boomers are at their peak of influence, and they possess great energy. In many ways, boomers are the antithesis of their parents' generation. Boomers often acted in ways that were contrary to the views of the GI generation. When the parents of boomers reached retirement age, they believed the world no longer belonged to them. Not so with boomers, who believe that it is never too late to change careers, the future, their appearance, or to reinvent themselves.

During the Great Recession, beginning mid-2007 with the bursting of the housing bubble until at least 2011, boomers lost jobs, watched their retirement funds shrink, and saw their home values take a "nose dive." Even today, in the aftermath of the Great Recession, many boomers face the difficult challenge of rebuilding a secure financial future. While there may be many disillusioned individual boomers, as a generation, they did not lose hope. Boomers have always been optimistic, believing that they could change the world. Boomers were the generation that fought to expand civil rights, protested the Vietnam War, participated in the women's liberation movement, encouraged environmental awareness, and helped change government.

While boomers are often associated with the festival at Woodstock and rock and roll music, it is helpful to put these two cultural experiences in perspective. First, approximately five hundred thousand people attended the famous musical event in Bethel, New York, in August 1969, a very small fraction of the total boomer generation. Obviously, a very small percentage of boomers actually attended Woodstock, and not all of the event participants were boomers. Second, the early leaders in rock and roll music were not members of the boomer generation. Rather, early icons of rock and roll (from Elvis Presley to the Beatles and the Rolling Stones) were part of the silent generation, the generation that preceded boomers. Perhaps the reason boomers are so closely associated with rock and roll is not only because it is their music of choice, but also because large numbers in that generation bought vinyl rock and roll albums.

Boomers do not fit every description, interest, habit, plan, or activity often attributed to them by the media. But there are some things that can be said about *most* boomers. For example, the concept of anti-aging has captured the interest of many of today's boomers, making them a huge market for products such as nutritional supplements, fad diets, fitness centers, hair color, and anti-wrinkle creams and lotions. Boomers are reluctant to let go of the illusion of youth. They will do nearly everything possible to keep themselves looking and acting youthful. They do not want to grow older, so they deny the veracity of their own aging. They see getting old as an option, rather than a reality. As boomers grow older, they may redefine old age and the concepts normally associated with aging.

Boomers do not identify with the labels around aging and old age. They do not see themselves as "retirees," even if they are retired. Nor do they think of themselves as being "old," as "seniors," "senior citizens," or "elderly." Although recent studies have shown that "older adult" is a more preferable term for older people among the American public, and some leading-edge boomers are a bit more comfortable with the term "older adult," many boomers aren't very accepting of this label. (For more information on reframing aging and ageism, see www.frameworksinstitute.org.) But, then, why should they be? The majority of boomers are still in their fifties and sixties; by today's standards, they are middle-age adults. While AARP and other organizations have lowered their age of membership to fifty or fifty-five years of age, boomers are not yet ready to assume the mantle of old age!

Boomers have an unwavering determination not to get old. As more boomers stay active, vibrant, and keep on working, they will change perceptions about being old. As life spans continue to expand, boomers face the challenge of increasing their health spans, which are the years of their lives when they can expect to be in good health and free from serious or chronic illness. Given time, however, boomers will face some of the same challenges related to health and aging that their parents faced.

Boomer Cohorts

To better understand boomers, it may be helpful to divide this generation into two separate groups or cohorts: leading-edge boomers (born 1946–1954) and trailing-edge boomers (born 1955–1964).[2] Because of the social, economic, and political influences taking place in the world during those years, boomers had different experiences.

Leading-edge boomers (who now range in age from early sixties to early seventies) are often associated with individualism, experimentation, anti-war activities, and civil rights movements. They tend to lean more to the "left of center" socially, politically, and religiously.

Trailing-edge boomers (who now range in age from mid-fifties to early sixties) are most often associated with general cynicism, less optimism, and fewer opportunities. As young adults, trailing-edge boomers were shaped by economic decline, a tight labor market, and the "Jesus Movement." They tend to lean more to the "right of center" socially, politically, and religiously.

Seeing boomers as the "new seniors" is a reference to the leading-edge boomers. Leading-edge boomers are experiencing the greatest challenges in their generation as a result of the forces of aging. They are experiencing the greatest physical changes, career changes, and the "empty nests." They are having the cataract surgeries and knee and hip replacements. They are suffering from chronic illnesses and obesity. They are dealing with their own health challenges or those of a spouse or partner. High cholesterol and high blood pressure are controlled by medications, and hearing loss now requires a hearing aid or two. If they haven't already retired, they are dreaming about retirement or transitioning to part-time work. Trailing-edge boomers, on the other hand, are experiencing their intimate relationships being tested and the challenges of midlife with career stagnation or advancement, parenthood, and aging parents.

Boomers and Retirement

While some boomers have retired, it is anticipated that many boomers will work longer with partial and/or delayed retirement. A number of factors are reinforcing this activity, including the increase of less physically strenuous, but more technically advanced work, which combines to intermingle work, education, retraining, and leisure. Further, boomers as a group do not appear to be saving enough money to be able to retire for twenty to thirty years. In addition to the fact that many boomers can't afford to retire, other reasons for changes in retirement for boomers include:

- They have continuing career interests.
- They want to stay productive.

- Work gives life meaning.
- Health-care needs and costs make work necessary.
- A decline in traditional pensions necessitates delayed retirement.
- Mandatory retirement has been eliminated for most jobs.

Rising life expectancy and poor economic conditions will force many boomers to keep working well beyond the "normal" retirement years. The shift to less physically demanding work, technical adaptions in work to accommodate disabilities at every age, opportunities for retraining, financial need, and better health status foretell a dramatic change in retirement plans for boomers.

Many boomers will "retire" to get a break, rest, and get ready for a new phase of work life. For many boomers, retirement is a transition, rather than a destination. True retirement is going to get deferred until later in life as long as their health (or that of a spouse/partner or aging parent) is good, new technology doesn't overwhelm their mental abilities, changes in the workplace don't complicate life, and age discrimination in the workplace isn't an issue.

Boomers and the Church

Many church leaders become distressed because boomers, especially leading-edge boomers, do not participate in the senior-adult ministries of the church. They fail to recognize that boomers do not see themselves as older adults, and many, if not most, are still working or leading very busy lives.

It's also helpful for church leaders to remember that as a generation, boomers have largely avoided traditional religious structures and have sought spiritual guidance from many sources. Leading-edge boomers, who are generally more liberal, may have left the faith because of the conservative emphasis on religion. They may find the church, as an institution, lacking in acceptance of people and yielding itself to ancient myths and superstitions. While many boomers returned to the church when they had school-age children, now after their children have grown and taken responsibility for their own lives, many boomers reduce their participation in church.

Churches wanting to engage boomers in spiritual growth must keep in mind that relationships are very important to members of this generation. Churches must find ways of helping boomers build relationships with others, as well as growing in a deeper relationship with God through Jesus Christ. Churches must pay attention to what is going on in the lives of boomers and to listen carefully to what they are saying. Churches should target the times of transitions and milestones in the lives of boomers and their families.

Congregations wanting to be intentional in ministry with boomers will accept this generation for who they are and where they are in life. Boomers will not attend worship services or events out of obligation. Religious guilt has little bearing on most boomers. The church just might not be a priority in their lives. To involve boomers, congregations should encourage short-term events or classes. Regular participation may not mean "weekly." Because of busy schedules with work and family needs, boomers have limited time for participation.

Churches wanting to reach boomers should:

- offer a variety of entry points where boomers can meet others.
- develop activities that engage boomers for their own sakes, and not just activities for children and youth.
- provide opportunities for meaningful service and mission.
- schedule activities that nurture their spiritual lives (e.g., journaling, prayer, and meditation).
- form small groups and support systems, keeping in mind that boomers define themselves not by their age, but by their interests, causes, and careers.
- recognize that many boomers will be working well beyond the "normal" retirement age and may not be able to provide the same degree of volunteer service as previous generations of seniors.
- realize that boomers have a tendency to financially support a cause, rather than simply giving to the general fund of the local church.

Keep in mind that boomers, at this stage of their lives, do not think of themselves as older people and have little interest in the current design of most older-adult ministries. Rather than asking boomers to participate in an existing older-adult ministry, start a new group designed by boomers, specifically for boomers.

Conclusion

Psychosocial, biological, spiritual, and economic issues will have an impact on the well-being of aging boomers. How the church responds to the needs of aging boomers will determine the health and vitality of most congregations. Many congregations failed in their attempts to reach boomers when they were young, so it will be interesting to see if the church will be effective in reaching boomers as they grow old.

Churches could do a great service for boomers if they would help boomers reframe their image of aging and ageism. Congregations that advance a positive yet realistic image of aging will enrich not only the lives of boomers but people of all ages.

Many congregations are trying innovative approaches for reaching this generation. A good way for churches to break age-related stereotypes is to build intergenerational relationships. Such a ministry can be exciting and challenging for congregations.

For many congregations, intentional ministry with boomers offers new directions for ministry. What this ministry will look like in the years ahead is uncertain. It will, however, be as complex, different, and unique as this generation.

Intentional Ministry by, with, and for Older Adults

"The righteous flourish like the palm tree, and grow like a cedar in Lebanon . . . In old age they still produce fruit; they are always green and full of sap."

—Psalm 92:12, 14

Congregations, like our society, are experiencing an era of demographic transition. The current growth of our aging population is one of the most significant demographic trends in the history of the church. As a result of the longevity revolution, many churches are experiencing growing numbers of older members. Congregations are graying because people are living longer and fewer young people are turning to the church for spiritual development and faith formation. With a growing number of people in our society who identify themselves as having no religious identity or affiliation, older adults in the church are finding themselves growing in numbers.

As a result of these changes, congregational transformation in an age of demographic transition involves rethinking church vitality. If church leaders believe that only congregations with growing numbers of children, youth, and young people can help churches bring about congregational vitality, they are going to miss out on new opportunities for growth and vital ministry. Congregational transformation in an age of demographic transition involves reimagining congregational vitality and learning to appreciate the positive aspects and unique challenges of graying members and aging communities. It involves inviting and equipping older adults to be a vital part of the church and encouraging them to contribute to ministry in ways that enrich both the church and community.

Many congregations with large numbers of older people can and do experience congregational vitality. The aging stereotypes of decline, dementia, and dependence must be replaced with empowering values of independence, activity, well-being, and service. Replacing stereotypes and ageist attitudes with empowering values can help transform graying congregations into vital congregations.

Church leaders in vital congregations know that people of all ages are called to be faithful witnesses of God's love. Older adults, no less than people of other ages, who are equipped and empowered for ministry can help nurture congregational transformation. Congregations in this new age find creative ways of inviting older adults to remain a vital part of the church by making significant contributions to ministry.

Starting Intentional Ministry by, with, and for Older Adults

Suggestions for churches that want to start intentional older-adult ministries include the following:

1. **Form a leadership team.** Identify older adults who have a passion and a calling for older-adult ministries and form a leadership team for starting intentional ministries by, with, and for older adults. The leadership team should be made up of six to twelve people, depending upon the size of your congregation. Representatives of the leadership team should include a variety of lifestyles and life stages of older adults. In other words, do not form a leadership team of all men or all widows, unless, of course, your church membership is composed of only men or widows! Invite people of various experiences to be part of the team: men and women, married couples, singles, widows and widowers, divorced people, active members, and homebound members. Team members should reflect a cross section of the diversity of older adults in your community. You might also want to include as part of your team people of other ages who have a passion or calling in older-adult ministry.

2. **Gather information about older adults in your congregation.** Identify the needs and talents of the older

adults who are part of your church. Design a survey questionnaire that obtains information about the needs, talents, and concerns of older adults in your congregation and, if possible, in your community. (Information about creating a survey instrument is found in Appendix C. Several samples of various survey forms are in appendixes D, E, and F. Instructions for how to conduct a survey in your church are found in Appendix G.)

3. **Identify existing church ministries that already involve older adults.** Look at all the various ministries, activities, and programs in your congregation that older adults are participating in, such as: worship, Sunday school classes, leadership positions, committee membership, Sunday school teaching, women's and men's groups, Bible study, and prayer groups. Gain a clear picture of the way older adults are already involved as members of the church.

4. **Survey other churches and community agencies in your area.** Find out what other churches are doing related to their older-adult ministries. Identify what services are available for older adults in your community. Contact the area agencies on aging (www.n4a.org) to find out what services are available in your community. Know what services, resources, and ministries are available for older adults and their families in your community.

5. **Develop a shared vision.** After you have surveyed older adults in your church and community and have

gained a clear understanding of what ministries and programs your congregation and community already have available for meeting the needs and talents of older adults, begin meeting with your leadership team to develop a vision for intentional ministry by, with, and for older adults in your congregation. What must your congregation begin doing to better meet the needs of older adults? How might your congregation make a difference in their lives?

6. **Design an intentional older-adult ministry in your congregation**. While there are many ideas or models for ministry with older adults, which we will look at more closely in chapters 8 and 9, there are six common models for ministry in most congregations:

   a. **Adult Day-Care Ministry**—Sometimes referred to as a Sunny Day Club, adult day-care ministry provides a safe place for people with mild cognitive impairment (MCI) to spend the day at church, while the primary caregiver is free for the day to do other things.

   b. **Congregational Care Ministry**—This ministry provides practical and compassionate care support for frail older adults living alone, in assisted living facilities, or in nursing homes. It involves visitation, resource information and support, and the promotion of health and wellness. Parish nursing (or Faith Community Nursing) may be an integral part of the congregational care ministry team.

   c. **Service Ministry**—Older adults reach out to serve the needs of others by providing transportation, minor home maintenance and repair, home chore service, lawn care, wheelchair ramps, grocery shopping or other types of food ministry, mission opportunities, and engage in such national programs as Habitat for Humanity and Room in the Inn.

d. **Social Ministry**—This ministry brings older adults together for social engagement that includes fellowship and travel opportunities, lunches or dinners, recreation and games, and entertainment.

e. **Study Ministry**—Older adults enjoy learning, so they come together to study particular books of the Bible, participate in special study classes and Sunday school, form a book club, and engage in other enrichment opportunities.

f. **Support Group Ministry**—Older adults meet with others for support related to various concerns such as cancer survivor support, caregiver support, adult children of aging parents support, widow/widower support, and grief and loss support.

7. **Identify resources and key personnel.** The leadership team needs to identify the key personnel who will *champion* the ministry. Having the right people to champion the ministry is important in getting the job done. Teams or committees that plan without identifying the people who will champion (provide leadership for) the ministry will likely fail in realizing their goal. Teams must also identify the key resources needed for the success of the ministry.

8. **Where/When appropriate, involve other congregations and social service agencies in your ministry.** Don't feel that you must go it alone. Involve other congregations and community agencies and resources in your planning, promotion, and delivery.
9. **Implement your ministry.** Understand your goals and objectives and develop a process for implementing your ministry, including timelines, check points, and leadership responsibilities.
10. **Evaluate your ministry.** During and following a specific ministry or program event, you will want to evaluate the success and effectiveness of the ministry. Obtain information from both participants and leaders. Ask: "What went well? What did you learn? What could be improved?" Use information from the evaluation in developing new ministry opportunities.

Vital congregations will find creative ways of engaging, equipping, and empowering a growing older-adult population. Ministry should be more than a "maintenance ministry" for older adults. Faced with the reality of an aging society, growing congregations will not get bogged down by negative attitudes about aging. Instead, vital congregations will plan and equip older adults to grow as mature Christians and will empower them for Christian mission and service. Suggestions for churches with growing numbers of older adults who want to experience congregational vitality include:

Build on your strengths, not your weaknesses. If you don't have a congregation filled with children, youth, or young adults, know who is there. If your church is situated in an area with more retired people than young people, your strength in ministry rests with midlife and older adults. Don't feel guilty or downtrodden for not having young people in your congregation. Plan ministry that intentionally engages older adults in faith development and in mission and service. Stay open to new ways of reaching children, youth, and young people, if possible; but don't lose sight of your strengths for ministry: older adults.

Form a Leadership Team. Identify people who have a passion and a calling for older-adult ministries and form a team. Then begin to identify the needs and talents of older adults in your church and community. Survey the older adults in your congregation and community to identify their needs and talents. With your team, develop a shared vision that engages, equips, and empowers older adults for ministry.

Follow your mission statement. For example, the mission statement for older-adult ministries (as well as for children's ministries, youth ministries, and adult ministries) in The United Methodist Church is to *make disciples of Jesus Christ for the transformation of the world.* Your church's mission statement may be different. However, whatever your church's mission is, guide your older-adult ministries with the mission of your church firmly implanted in your vision.

Empower lay leadership teams. Older-adult ministry is not something that is done by a pastor to senior adults or by a volunteer leader for older adults. Rather, it is a ministry by, with, and for older adults. Such a ministry seeks to equip and empower other adults for ministry. Older-adult ministry is, in most situations, a ministry of the laity. Clergy should certainly support and may help shepherd and guide the ministry, but it is a ministry of the laity. Vital congregations empower lay leadership teams with older adults who provide caregiving ministries, mission and service opportunities, and small-group ministries. Invite lay leadership teams to visit homebound and nursing home residents and to take Holy Communion to them. Lay leadership teams can help hold one another accountable in growing as Christians, and they can model spiritual maturity for others.

Use lifestyle, not age, as the determining factor for ministry. Chronological age is not important in ministry with people at midlife and beyond. Rather, lifestyle issues and concerns are more important to ministry. For example, grandparenting concerns are not just for people who are retired. Grandparents can be as young as late thirties and early forties. What common concerns do all grandparents, of whatever age, experience? You may want to create your small-group ministry around common interests, concerns, or careers.

Develop various ministry options. Recognize that one ministry type does not meet the needs of all older adults. Some older adults will enjoy meeting together for a weekly or monthly noon luncheon and program, while other older adults would rather be part of a mission team or take part in a community service project. Some older adults will be available during the day; others will be working and available only at night or on weekends. Some older adults will need caregiving services, while others can be care providers. Some older adults will enjoy singing old familiar hymns, while others enjoy singing newer praise songs. Remember: no two older adults are exactly alike; therefore, no single ministry will reach everyone.

Foster intergenerational ministry and lifelong learning. Create opportunities for intentional intergenerational ministry with young people and older adults. Help older adults to become active listeners and faith sharers for young people in your congregation and community. Also find ways that older adults can continue to learn and grow in faith and life. People who age well often have growing relationships with younger people and enjoy opportunities for learning from others. For example, computer skills are increasingly needed to access community information and resources. Many older adults who wish to stay informed, to obtain needed services, or to keep up with the digital age so they can email children and grandchildren may require training on computers or smart phones. Young people can generally provide this technology assistance. Invite older adults to invest in the lives of young people and in lifelong learning.

Make your church facilities inviting and accessible. Keep in mind the changing needs of people as they grow older. Restrooms should be accessible; lighting needs to be bright enough and font sizes large enough for people to be able to read; acoustics and sound systems should allow all people to be able to hear clearly; and signs should be available for older adults to easily identify where to go upon entering the building. Plan Bible study groups for older adults at a variety of different times, including during daylight hours for those who have retired and during the late afternoons, early evenings, or on weekends for older adults who are still working. Create an atmosphere of radical hospitality that is warm, friendly, and inviting for all midlife and older adults.

Use appropriate language. Use appropriate language when describing older adults. Just because a person is older and/or retired, does not mean that he or she is "elderly." Remove the term "shut-ins" from your vocabulary. "Shut-in" is not an appropriate word to describe people who are unable to attend church services. Instead, use the terms "home-bound" or "home-centered" to describe people on your prayer and visitation lists. Never refer to people as "handicapped" or "disabled." Instead, say, "people with handicapping conditions" or "people with a disability." Sensitivity in our use of language concerning older adults and other adults is important to convey in our congregations. As a church leader, set an example for the use of language and help people in your congregation do the same.

The Role of the Church

In a culture that devalues aging, many older people may feel useless, that they are too old to be of service, or that they are not needed. And many church leaders believe that the leadership of the church should be turned over to younger people, in addition to holding the ageist belief that the church should reflect a more "youthful" demographic. As a result, many older adults are afraid to express their thoughts or to suggest what needs to be addressed for their own age group in the church.

Only when the church rejects our culture's ageist script can older adults truly begin to become all that God intends. Every age and stage of life has its strengths, from physical resilience to historical perspective. Along with growing older come new experiences, new concerns, and new questions, all of which demand new approaches to church ministry. While the church is grateful for the financial contributions made by older adults, it must also recognize that the wisdom, faith, and experience of older adults are also of great importance to the future of the church.

Empowered older adults are making meaningful contributions to their communities, serving as valuable wisdom-givers to their families, and providing historical grounding to young people. Churches that are intentional in older-adult ministry are experiencing older adults who are providers, not just recipients, of the church's ministry.

Equipping older adults for living out their Christian discipleship in other significant ways, even when health and physical strength decline, is an important role for the church. Helping older adults recapture a vision for Christ-centered service and enabling them to identify and develop their spiritual gifts is not only essential for older adults' well-being, it is vital for both church and community.

The role of the church in creating intentional ministry by, with, and for older adults takes on new urgency in this time of demographic transition. Important new directions for the church are to:

- help senior adults know that they are valued, respected, and needed in ministry. How we age often depends on the way we internalize the images of growing old. The church must condemn ageism in society and within its own walls and affirm and challenge older adults in ministry. It is important for a graying congregation to recognize that it is not an "old" church, but a church that is blessed by having many older members.

- provide senior adults with new opportunities for learning and service, knowing that older adults are active participants in contributing to the church's life and mission.

- help senior adults find meaning and purpose in the later years, knowing that aging can entail a "crisis of meaning." In later life, older adults begin to wonder if their life has made a difference to anyone—if it has meaning.

- affirm and challenge older adults, acknowledging both the blessings and the losses of later life and recognizing that interdependence, not independence, is a way of enhancing the dignity and worth of all people as children of God.

- develop structures for intentional ministry that encourage and facilitate the contributions and faith development of older adults. Aging demands the attention of the entire church.

- offer ministries that provide spiritual nurture and healing for all seniors: Go-Goes, Slow-Goes, and No-Goes. The church recognizes that spiritual growth of the aging person is affected by the community and affects the community.

- provide support systems for grief and loneliness. We are all growing older, not just as individuals, but as members of a faith community.

S.E.N.I.O.R.S. Ministry Model

Churches that provide intentional ministry with older adults recognize that there is no older-adult population. Instead, there are multiple older-adult populations, and each one is different. No one ministry type reaches all the older adults in a congregation. Not only are there many different age cohorts, from 55 to 105, but there are married couples, widows, divorced, never married and always single, healthy-active, frail-elderly, homebound, and residents in continuing care retirement communities, just to name a few. As people grow older, they generally become less alike, not more so. Therefore, their needs and talents and their likes and dislikes are all vastly different.

Unfortunately, some congregations believe that if they engage in ministry by, with, and for older adults, they will soon have no congregation left. They may not realize that a congregation filled with older adults does not necessarily mean that the church is dead or dying. Congregations may need to rethink and refocus their priorities for ministry. In doing so, many congregations have come to understand that the older-adult population provides tremendous potential for vital ministry.

Older adults want to continue contributing to the well-being of future generations, and they desire to feel valued because of their contributions. Congregations that are intentional in their older-adult ministry realize that the wealth of experience, wisdom, and faith that often abounds in older people should not be lost or go unused. If churches do not see the challenges and opportunities for intentional older-adult ministry, this growing population will see the church as nothing more than a place for life-cycle ceremonies (i.e., baptisms, confirmations, weddings, and funerals) and not as a sacred community of meaning.

A helpful way for congregations wanting to develop intentional ministry by, with, and for older adults is the S.E.N.I.O.R.S. ministry model. The S.E.N.I.O.R.S. ministry model identifies seven key areas that provide for the development of intentional ministry. The seven areas are **S**pirituality, **E**nrichment, **N**utrition (health & wellness), **I**ntergenerational, **O**utreach, **R**ecreation, and **S**ervice. The S.E.N.I.O.R.S. ministry model is an effective tool for making certain that congregational ministry with older adults is intentional and comprehensive. Note the outline below.

S–Spirituality: Plan and develop Bible study groups; prayer groups; adult religious education classes; life review classes; spiritual retreats; guided journaling classes; worship participation; rituals to acknowledge life transitions dealing with change, separation, loss, and new commitments; healing services; and seminars on end-of-life issues.

E–Enrichment: Plan and develop classes and small groups relevant to the specific learning needs and concerns of older adults. You might focus on community issues and current affairs; computers and technology; financial, legal, and health concerns; wills and advance directives; fine arts such as painting and music; travel and field trips; and literacy programs.

N–Nutrition (Health & Wellness): Plan and develop a parish nurse ministry (Faith Community Nursing), congregational health-care ministry, low-impact aerobics and other physical fitness classes, health fairs, and cooking classes.

I–Intergenerational: Plan and develop opportunities for coaching, mentoring, and tutoring future generations. Involve all ages in worship, study classes, and spiritual life retreats. Encourage participants of all ages in service and mission projects.

O–Outreach: Plan and develop ways for older adults to reach out to other older adults who do not have a church home, to older adults living in nursing homes, and to other people of all ages; start an adult day-care ministry; provide respite care and meals; and offer minor home maintenance ministry.

R–Recreation: Plan and develop social activities for health and fun living; conduct golf, fishing, and other sports outings; attend ball games together. Encourage walking, hiking, and camping/RV activities. Invite older adults to participate in gardening, flower arranging, and card and board games.

S–Service: Plan and develop opportunities for older adults to engage in service projects, including short-term mission projects, community projects, respite-care ministry, prison ministry, meals on wheels delivery, visitation ministry, transportation ministry, and home chore ministry.

Ten Tips for Successful S.E.N.I.O.R.S. Ministry

1. Develop a shared vision for older-adult ministry. The leadership team should have a well-thought-out and planned vision for intentional ministry by, with, and for older adults. The vision plan should meet the needs of older adults.

2. Make the older-adult ministry part of a specific organization in the church. The older-adult ministry should be structured and not exist outside the official organization of the church. The ministry should be part of the overall ministry of the church.

3. Support the older-adult ministry in the church budget. Provide older-adult ministry a line item in the budget. Make funds available to meet ministry needs.

4. Assess the needs and talents of older adults. Conduct an older-adult survey in the church and community to identify the needs and talents of older adults.

5. Keep records. Record activities of the ongoing ministry for future reference. Maintain records of emergency contacts for older adults.

6. Ensure that leaders are available. Complete background checks on all leaders. Leaders need to be willing to champion specific older-adult ministries, depending upon their experience, knowledge, talent, and interest.

7. Provide training related to specific older-adult ministries and in areas such as first aid, CPR, and elder abuse awareness.

8. Determine what resources are available in the community—whether through social service agencies, government agencies, or other churches.
9. Reach out to older adults and their families in the community.
10. Evaluate regularly to assess strengths and to discover areas of weakness.

Congregational leaders desiring to be in ministry by, with and for older adults will want to use the "Local Church Assessment S.E.N.I.O.R.S. Ministry Model." This instrument invites church leaders to identify all ministries related to the S.E.N.I.O.R.S. ministry model and the three phases of retirement (active, passive, and final). For example, identify in each box all the areas of ministry related to spirituality with each phase of retirement. Then identify in each box all the areas of ministry related to enrichment with each phase of retirement, and so on until you complete the "Local Church Assessment S.E.N.I.O.R.S. Ministry Model."

The "Local Church Assessment S.E.N.I.O.R.S. Ministry Model" is valuable for any size congregation, including small-, medium- and large-membership congregations. As you use the assessment tool, it is important that you don't become overwhelmed by the many possibilities for ministry or that you feel bad about not having ministry in certain areas. The assessment tool is useful for identifying the ministry your church is already engaged in and to ascertain what other ministry areas you might begin to address.

Local Church Assessment S.E.N.I.O.R.S. Ministry Model

Using the chart below, identify your church ministry in each area of the S.E.N.I.O.R.S. Ministry Model that has an impact on the three phases of retirement. In each box below, name the particular ministries that will meet the needs of the various life stages of the retirement years.

S.E.N.I.O.R.S. Ministry Assessment	Go-Goes Active Phase	Slow-Goes Passive Phase	No-Goes Final Phase
Spirituality			
Enrichment			
Nutrition/ Wellness			
Intergenerational			
Outreach			
Recreation			
Service			

Conclusion

When older adults see little interest directed at them by the church, they gradually lose their sense of having value and worth, and this dampens and diminishes their faith and spiritual development. Congregations and church leaders that help energize and reignite the spiritual fires of faith in older adults will experience a generation that takes seriously its role in helping to make disciples of Jesus for the transformation of the world.

Older adults have a vital role in helping preserve the traditions of the church: the faith, the worship, the teaching. Whether young people participate in the life of the church or not, older adults have a responsibility to keep the faith alive. As Christians, we must discern carefully between preserving that which is truly the will of God and that which is of our own making. It is important for leaders of older-adult ministries to lift up older adults as keepers of the faith and to help congregations understand and appreciate this unique role. However, it is equally clear that the role of the church is to call into question the "preservation of past traditions" when God's call is for change.

Older adults cannot become too oriented to the past or long to go back to the "good old days." Older adults can, as keepers of the faith, model what it means to be people who learn, grow, and change, and do so successfully. They can help the church preserve what is good and just and loving. They can help the church live a Christ-centered existence because they are helping maintain and preserve the love of God within the community. When older adults are open to

God's will and are engaged in the task as a growing, learning, teaching people, they are better able to be faithful to the task of keepers of the faith. Traditions, rituals, and even our understanding of God's Word may change completely. Older adults who are growing in faith may not only help bring about needed change in the church, but they may be the instigators and provocateurs who enable such change.

CHAPTER 6

Organizing for Intentional Ministry in the Local Church

"Honor your father and your mother, so that your days may be long in the land that the Lord your God is giving you."

—Exodus 20:12

According to *The Book of Discipline* of The United Methodist Church, the mission of the church is *to make disciples of Jesus Christ for the transformation of the world.* (*The Book of Discipline of The United Methodist Church, 2016*, page 91). As we think about the church's mission, let's look at several questions related to older adults.

- How can a local church reach out to older adults in its community? Many older adults in any community are without a church home and have no relationship with God through Jesus Christ.

- How can the church help older adults experience a new or renewed relationship with God through Jesus Christ? Some older adults have been members of the church for years and may have become complacent in their faith. Others are experiencing life-changing challenges and transitions that influence their faith maturity, while still other older adults may have deep scars as a result of being hurt or victimized by the church years ago.

- What are the best ways to help nurture older adults in the Christian faith? Some older adults enjoy small-groups such as Sunday school classes, women's or men's groups, and Bible study groups. Others are reluctant joiners and prefer more social activities and fellowship time.

- How can the local church best support older adults as they live and act as faithful disciples in the community? Many older adults may no longer be able to drive and now need help with transportation; they may have other unmet needs. Or, after raising their own children, many older adults are now finding it necessary to raise their grandchildren, and they wonder if they have the energy, skills, and knowledge for such an undertaking.

The traditional response to the above questions by many churches over the years has been a combination of adult Sunday school class, worship service, and monthly social luncheon/program. Pastors and volunteers provided pastoral and congregational care for older adults in need. When crises came, the church responded to meet the needs.

But a wider vision of older-adult ministry in our world today holds that such activities are the *minimal base* for programming. Today, with more people living longer and with many more older adults in our congregations, growing older becomes more complicated and challenging. Intentional older-adult ministry in the local church requires that church leaders strategize ways to further Christian discipleship among older adults.

Today's church leaders recognize that the church must address the *physical* needs of older adults (e.g., transportation, nutrition, health care, caregiving, and livable communities, etc.), and many congregations are providing ministry in these important areas. But the church cannot disregard the *emotional* needs of older adults (e.g., depression, loss of self-esteem and self-worth, isolation, loneliness, and fears), and it is also called to add the *spiritual* dimension to its ministry among older adults. The church is called to empower and equip older adults in Christian discipleship. Church leaders should feel free to design ministry with many options for enrichment in Christian faith and practice—mixing social services and intentionally religious activities that put Christ in their midst. The church must offer a total ministry—body, mind, and spirit—for meeting the needs of the whole person.

Many churches are finding that older adults themselves want to be involved in an intentional ministry by, with, and for older adults. Churches often begin by forming a fellowship group with officers, regular meetings, and a varied program of activities. They might start a monthly luncheon fellowship with a program. Sometimes they engage in a ministry around a particular need, such as transportation ministry for older adults who no longer drive or a respite-care for family caregivers. The amount of organization a church needs for older-adult ministry depends upon many things: the number of older adults who are involved, the kinds of needs to be served, the readiness of the congregation to meet the needs, available financial resources, and the leaders available for the task.

All ministries that have an impact on the lives of older adults should be organized under one central area of ministry. Each separate ministry entity (transportation, fellowship meals, caregiving, visitation, etc.) is therefore known and accountable to the overall mission and vision of older-adult ministry. The reason for this type of organization is so that with each entity, a clear understanding can be realized regarding the total older-adult ministry.

The ministry may choose a name for itself, rather than being called "older-adult" or "senior-adult" ministries. While there are hundreds of different names used by churches for older-adult ministries, some common names include: "Fifty-Plus Club, " "XYZ (Extra Years of Zest) Club," "JOY (Just Older Youth) Group," "M&Ms" (Mature and Methodist), "Sage Club," "New Horizons," "Fresh Horizons," "Encore Ministries," "Three Score and More," and "Keenagers."

While all older adults of the church should indeed be part of one fellowship, there are reasons for various groups, teams, and ministries. For example, although the older-adult ministry may include a monthly luncheon and program, not all older adults will be able or want to attend. Some older adults cannot attend the monthly meal gathering because they are the primary caregivers for a spouse or partner; they are working full or part time; they are volunteering for "meals on wheels" during lunch time; or their diets do not permit eating the type of food being served. Churches must remember to engage in more than one type of ministry since a single ministry program will not reach or be effective for all older adults.

Getting Started—The Role of the Leader

If you are the pastor, coordinator, or team leader for older-adult ministries in your local church, you will want to become familiar with your role. The primary task for the local church leader of older-adult ministries is to assist the local church in its ministry by, with, and for older adults. The leader is responsible for coordinating the ministry, chairing the leadership team meetings, helping to plan for ministry, overseeing the work of various ministry teams, and making certain ministry is carried out. The leader does not do all the work of the leadership team; rather, the leader facilitates and coordinates the work of others. He or she helps committees and teams of older adults in setting up plans and getting a new ministry with older adults started. The leader assists in any way necessary toward carrying forward ministry by, with, and for older adults.

The leader for older-adult ministries should be an articulate person who communicates well with others. He or she must be an advocate on behalf of the needs and concerns of older adults. The leader needs to be involved in the life of the local church and be growing in the Christian faith. The leader should be knowledgeable about older-adult concerns and aging issues and open-minded concerning the diversity among older adults. Finally, the leader should be a person who can enlist and encourage others to participate in events and programs and is capable of acquiring resources needed for ministry.

Organize for Intentional Ministry— The Leadership Team

As indicated in the previous chapter, the older-adult ministry leadership team should be composed of six to twelve people, depending upon the size of the congregation. The majority of the team members should be older adults. Represented on the leadership team should be the different types of older adults in the congregation: women, men, various races and ethnicities, as well as people who are single, married, widowed, and divorced. While many of the team members will be active and living in their own homes, consider inviting older adults to join the team who are homebound and who reside in assisted living facilities and nursing homes. Make certain the leadership team reflects the variety of older adults in the community in order to have a broad perspective of the needs and concerns of older adults represented.

The older-adult ministry leadership team should have a team leader or chairperson, a vice chairperson, and a recording secretary. Other members of the leadership team should be available to help champion (lead) the development of specific ministry areas and to assist in planning the goals and objectives of particular ministry areas.

The older-adult ministry leadership team should be in every church, regardless of a congregation's membership size. The small-membership church may believe there are not enough people to warrant the creation of an older-adult ministry leadership team to advance the cause of an intentional ministry by, with, and for older adults. Do not dismiss the possibility of an older-adult ministry leadership team simply because you believe your church membership is not large enough. Through investigation, you may learn that there are older adult needs and concerns in your community that would create opportunities for older-adult ministry. Therefore, it may be helpful for you to expand your concept of an older-adult ministry leadership team by including people from outside your church and within your local community on the team.

If you do not believe that your congregation's membership is large enough to develop intentional ministry by, with, and for older adults, or if you feel that you do not have the necessary resources or personnel, you can still engage in this vital ministry. You do not need to do ministry alone. An older-adult ministry leadership team can be developed with leaders from several churches, such as a multiple-church charge, a circuit, or a cluster of churches from the same community. Where there are older adults, there is a need for ministry.

The Planning Process for the Leadership Team

The following four important steps will assist the older-adult ministry leadership team in the planning process:

Step 1: Define the Problem. The older-adult ministry leadership team will want to identify the specific needs of older adults in the church and community. The team will also want to identify specific needs of other ages in the church and community with whom older adults can engage in ministry. Remember, the leadership team is developing an intentional ministry by, with, and for older adults, not just a ministry *to* older adults.

The team must then prioritize the needs and suggestions for ministry and ask basic questions, such as: "What are the needs and talents of older adults in the church? Which areas of concern are of greater interest to the team and to the church? Are resources available to help meet the needs? What goals and objectives need to be put in place for guiding the ministry? What steps need to be taken to ensure the success of the ministry?"

Step 2: Develop the Specific Ministry or Activity. The leadership team plans the appropriate ministry or activity to meet the specific needs of the proposed objectives. An excellent program can fail miserably when the plans are unrealistic. Goal-setting procedures can help avoid such problems. Ask these questions: "What do we want to happen? How can we best get that done? What results should come from it?"

There may be both short- and long-term goals. A plan for a year's program to get all people over seventy involved in an older-adult group is a long-term goal. A one-day ministry of building a ramp at a home of a frail, elderly person is a short-term goal. Goals and objectives for a short-term program or project must be stated as clearly and carefully as those for a long-term program or project, so that both the leaders and the older adults participating know the desired results.

When you have reached a decision about what you want to do, determine costs and set a budget. Few congregations plan to undergird older-adult ministries in their church budgets. While churches usually include children's programs and youth activities in their church budgets, they often think that older adults should pay extra for their activities. They may need help in understanding that many older adults do not have the financial resources. Sometimes, local church finance committees are composed of older-adult members who may have adequate financial resources and fail to recognize the needs of others. Or, they may believe that to add another line item to the church budget for older adults is self-serving or unnecessary.

The older-adult ministry leadership team may find itself having to advocate for the financial support of the church on behalf of the needs of older adults. Do not grow weary in this task and do not apologize for needing to help meet the needs of a growing population of older adults. There are likely many older adults in your church and community who do not have the necessary financial resources to participate in various ministry opportunities. You might approach the church finance committee with a financial scale of needs, showing the most you would need and the least you could operate with.

In addition to your local church, other ways of receiving additional monies to fund older-adult ministry includes applying for grant funding. Money might be available through your church denominational structures such as your district, synod, diocese, or conference. In addition, there may be foundations that provide funding in your local community, or grants may be available through a state agency. Finally, look to local businesses in the community for support. There may be several businesses that would be willing to provide financial support for older-adult ministry if they can market or advertise their business or product.

Once you have obtained funding, list the tasks to be performed and select leaders. Begin the process by asking these questions: "What resources are needed for the ministry? What steps must be taken to realize the success of this ministry? What is the start date and timeline for completion?" As your team works to answer these questions, it will then be necessary for someone from the leadership team to champion the ministry. The leader who agrees to champion the specific ministry will act as the program ministry manager, making certain that all tasks are completed, resources are secured, and the program ministry is carried out successfully.

Step 3: Implement the Program Ministry. The champion, working with other members of the leadership team, must recruit volunteers and, if necessary, obtain necessary resources. The ministry must be marketed or advertised throughout the church and community, and participants need to be invited. Remember, the champion does not do all the work in implementing the program ministry, but manages or oversees—*champions*—the work of others. A team must be formed to carry out the program ministry. The champion's responsibility is to enlist the support of the church and community and to invite others to be part of the program ministry team.

At this point, it may become necessary for the champion to refine the program ministry proposal. Again, working with the leadership team, the champion brings before the team any suggested changes in the proposal prior to implementing the program. Refinement of the program ministry proposal may come about as a result of changes in related resources, personnel, or budget needs.

After refining and fine-tuning the proposal and establishing evaluation procedures, it is time for the program ministry to be implemented.

Step 4: Evaluate the Program Ministry. Prior to the completion, or immediately following the completion of the program ministry, it is important to do an evaluation. The leadership team needs to collect, organize, and interpret data. Questions to ask of all participants and leaders might include the following: "What did you learn? What went well? What could be improved?" These three simple questions can get to the heart of any good evaluation.

Evaluation of the effectiveness of the program ministry will help the leadership team and the church know if the ministry is to be continued, changed for improvement, dropped altogether for the time being, or stopped indefinitely. Using the collected data from the evaluation process, the leadership team can begin the planning process again or start a new program ministry.

Local Church Ministry Review

Periodically, every congregation should review its ministry, and this is no less true for older-adult ministries. If we are not intentional in our efforts, we may find older adults are less active in their faith development and more willing to "sit on the sidelines" than be fully engaged in Christian ministry.

The following questions are intended to help local churches evaluate the effectiveness of their overall ministry by, with, and for older adults:

1. *Is it intentional?*
   The number of older adults in our society and our congregations is growing. These people, usually identified as either retired or sixty-five years of age and older, have special needs, concerns, and potential. On a regular basis, each local congregation should survey the church membership and take a "needs and talents" assessment and resource inventory of its older-adult members (*see Appendixes C, D, E, F, and G*). Such action can provide the local church some certainty that it is taking the necessary steps that give vision to intentional ministry by, with, and for older adults.

2. *Does it empower older adults for life and ministry?*
   Older people want to be active in the church and community. If they are being empowered and equipped, they are growing in greater understanding of what

it means to live a Christian life. Their leadership is solicited, welcomed, and used. They are encouraged to take charge of their own lives and are given primary responsibility for developing, implementing, and coordinating a ministry by, with, and for older adults. They are engaged in helping to meet the needs of others both within the church and in their communities.

3. *Is the church free of barriers for all participants?*

Remove physical, psychological, social, and economic barriers so that older adults are better able to participate fully in the life and activities of the church. Some examples include: clear signs are visible throughout the church building; ramps are in place for wheelchairs; restrooms are accessible; classrooms and sanctuary are well lighted; hearing devices are available for the hearing-impaired; and programs are made available during the light of day.

4. *Does the church reach out to older adults?*

For ministry to purposefully reach out to all older people, churches should include evangelism, worship, Bible study, outreach, pastoral/congregational care, small groups, Christian education, and mission and service opportunities as program offerings for older adults. On the church website, photos of older adults engaged in ministry are displayed on the masthead, not simply photos of children and youth. In addition, the church website should include a link to the church's various ministries by, with, and for older adults. Older adults with changing lifestyle needs or who have moved into the community and are looking for a church home may be computer and internet savvy. Your presence on the internet and your ministry prominently displayed on your church's website can be helpful for many older adults as they explore your ministry by, with, and for older adults. Emails, newsletters, telephone calls, visitations, and regular mailings are just some of the efforts that need to be made to communicate with older people.

5. *Are concerns of aging included in the liturgy?*

The joys, celebrations, fears, frustrations, losses, and dreams of older adults need to be included as an integral part of litanies, prayers, hymns, and sermons. Aging challenges and transitions experienced by older adults should be regularly highlighted in sermons and newsletter articles. Milestones passed and goals achieved should be celebrated. Older adults should be encouraged to share their faith and to take an active role in worship services. Rites of passage (such as retirement) and rituals (such as a house blessing) should be provided for the support and ministry of older adults. New rituals for transitions in the lives of older adults should be developed (such as a ritual for older adults moving from their home to a residence in a continuing care retirement community).

6. *Does the ministry provide opportunities for continuous spiritual and personal growth?*

Bible study groups, healing services, and prayer groups are just some of the efforts that should be made available for spiritual guidance. Opportunities for various types of classes, seminars, workshops, and support groups (such as widow/widower support groups, grief and loss support groups, and grandparents raising grandchildren support groups) could be provided to help with life transitions and to enhance learning skills.

7. *Are opportunities provided for companionship and socialization?*
   Older adults need to be able to enrich their lives through fellowship with others.

   Older adults should join together for a monthly luncheon and program. They should come together for game day at the church, to quilt or sew lap blankets, and to prepare food baskets for people in need. They should enjoy travel ventures and enrichment programs. Through planned activities and events, they will receive affection, respect, recognition, stimulation, and feelings of self-worth.

8. *Are many of the church's programs intergenerational?*
   Older adults have the opportunity to share their faith, experience, and knowledge with people of all ages. Likewise, they have the opportunity to learn from people of other ages. Plan intergenerational retreats for young and old each year. Invite multiple generations to participate in special Sunday school classes regularly. Encourage older people and young people to work together on various projects and exchange services with one another.

   Intergenerational programming with young people and older adults should provide information and resources that encourage learning and understanding for each age and stage of life. Listed below are some important elements to keep in mind when planning intergenerational programs:

- Aging is a natural progression in life.
- Aging is not a disease, morbid, or unnatural.
- Aging is not synonymous with death and dying.
- Each age and stage of life is full of unique potential.
- The older-adult population is a diverse group; no two older adults are exactly alike.
- Stereotypical thinking about older adults may be inaccurate.
- Stereotypical thinking about children and youth may be inaccurate.
- Children, youth, and older adults can learn from one another.
- God loves and blesses people of all ages.
- God calls people of all ages into Christian discipleship.

9. *Is the church community-minded and ecumenical?*
Older adults should be encouraged to become familiar with the programs and services of their local community and public agencies and, when possible, to be engaged in volunteer service. Social services should be known and used as needed by older adults. The ministry should reach out into the community to avail itself to the needs of older adults. Join with other congregations in mobilizing cooperative efforts to do what cannot be done separately.

10. *Does the ministry address concerns related to social policies and issues?*

The ministry should inform older adults about pending local, state, and national legislation, social policies, and other issues that may adversely affect their lives, as well as the lives of other people and generations. Form study groups, task forces, and/or committees and act as advocates to help combat social problems. Encourage older adults to engage in social justice and peace activities on behalf of others.

Intentional ministry by, with, and for older adults in a local church is a challenging and rewarding ministry. It is certainly more than the traditional adult Sunday school class, a monthly social, and ministry to the homebound or home-centered members.

Each local church is called upon to become aware of the needs and interests of older adults in the congregation and community and to assure a barrier-free environment in which older adults (and people with handicapping conditions) can function in spite of impairments. Developing intentional older-adult ministry requires congregations to recognize that older adults represent a creative human resource available to the church and to involve them in service to the community as people of experience, knowledge, wisdom, and faith.

Conclusion

Congregations that are intentional in ministry by, with, and for older adults will:

1. assure access to life maintenance for each person, including health services, mobility, personal security, and other personal services.
2. offer opportunities for life enrichment, including intellectual stimulation, social involvement, spiritual cultivation, and artistic pursuits.
3. encourage life reconstruction when necessary, including motivation and guidance in establishing new social networks following retirement or moving to a new location, serving roles in the community, enriching marriage, supporting grandparents raising grandchildren, and providing support groups for life-changing situations (e.g., divorce, death of spouse, cancer survivor, and retirement).
4. affirm life transcendence, including celebration of the meaning and purpose of life through worship, Bible study, personal reflection, and small-group life.

CHAPTER 7

Organizing for Intentional Ministry in the Conference

"Do not cast me off in the time of old age; do not forsake me when my strength is spent."
—PSALM 71:9

Older-adult ministries in the local church may be enhanced with the help of the resources and support of older-adult ministries on a conference (or denominational or judicatory) level. For example, some denominations have staff on the national level who, with advanced training and expertise, are charged with resourcing the needs of older-adult ministries in local churches. In addition, there may be teams or committees on a national or regional level who provide guidance and support to help resource local church leaders in the area of older-adult ministries.

Discipleship Ministries (formerly the General Board of Discipleship) provides resources for annual conferences, districts, and local church leaders in older-adult ministries. The United Methodist Church also has a Committee on Older Adult Ministries, which has representation from the various boards and agencies of the church, as well as older-adult representatives from the various regions of the church. The work of the committee is to serve as an advocate on behalf of older adults and to help resource older-adult ministries within The United Methodist Church.

Conference Committee on Older-Adult Ministries

In the past, the *Book of Resolutions* of The United Methodist Church highlighted the need for each annual conference to have a conference council on older-adult ministries. The language was permissive and invited conferences to consider the need for such a council.

For annual conferences to become intentional about our graying congregations and older-adult ministry, they need to develop a committee on older-adult ministries. What follows is a new, revised proposal for conferences that moves from a conference council on older-adult ministries format to that of a conference committee on older-adult ministries. This proposal is also suitable for other judicatory bodies to adapt and adopt.

1. In each annual conference there shall be a **conference committee on older adult ministries**. Its purpose shall be to strengthen and support older-adult ministries in

the local churches and districts of the annual confer-ence. For administrative purposes, the committee shall be related to an executive, administrative, or program body of the annual conference.

2. *Membership*—The majority of the membership of the committee shall be older adults; it will also include persons (regardless of age) who, because of their spe-cialized interests, education, training, and experience, have developed a passion for ministry with older adults. There shall be two members from each district, one lay-person and one clergy, selected by the district nomina-tions committee. There shall also be members at-large, nominated by the conference nominating committee and elected by the annual conference, to achieve racial, ethnic, and gender inclusiveness; and to assure partici-pation by persons with specialized interests, education, training, and experiences. The conference lay leader (or designee), the conference coordinator of older-adult ministries (if any), and a cabinet representative shall serve ex-officio, with vote.

3. *Meetings*—The committee shall meet at least twice a year and preferably quarterly. The committee shall elect its own officers and establish the necessary subcommit-tees and task forces to fulfill the committee's goals and objectives.

4. *Responsibilities*
   a. To initiate and support ministries, plans, activities and projects that are of particular interest to older adults.

b. To advocate on behalf of older adults and issues that impact the well-being of older adults.

c. To support and facilitate, where appropriate, the formation of older-adult caucuses.

d. To encourage and support the creation of networks among church leaders of older-adult ministries in each district and within the conference.

e. To identify the needs, concerns, and potential contributions of older adults in the annual conference and its districts.

f. To cooperate with the boards and agencies of the annual conference in receiving and making recommendations to provide for the needs of older adults in the annual conference and within the life of The United Methodist Church.

g. To educate and keep before the annual conference and its districts the lifelong process of aging with emphases on the quality of life, intergenerational understandings, and faith development.

h. To serve as a focal point for supplying information and guidance on older-adult ministries within the annual conference and its districts.

i. To support the development of resources that will undergird older-adult ministries within the annual conference and its districts.

j. To resource and equip congregations for intentional ministries by, with, and for older adults.

k. To provide leadership for district workshops and seminars with clergy and laity on aging issues and older-adult ministries.

The Tennessee Annual Conference

In The United Methodist Church, annual conferences (regional judicatory bodies) may also have a staff person and a team or committee that provides training, support, and resources for leaders of older-adult ministry within the annual conference.

Within the Tennessee Conference, there exists the Golden Cross Foundation, an extension ministry that provides funding for local churches in the area of older-adult ministries. The Golden Cross Foundation receives funding from financial gifts given to the organization through the annual Golden Cross Offering in local churches and from another foundation, the McKendree Village Foundation. The Golden Cross Foundation operates with the support of a board of directors and an executive director.

The Tennessee Conference also supports the work of the conference committee on older-adult ministries, which sponsors an annual leadership training day, a spiritual retreat for seniors, and Christmas at Beersheba Springs (a conference retreat center). The conference committee is made up of volunteer leaders from across the conference, including a chairperson, recording secretary, representatives from the various districts, and resource personnel with expertise in older-adult ministries.

In the fall of 2014, representatives from the Golden Cross Foundation and the Tennessee Conference Committee on Older-Adult Ministries formed an advisory team and engaged in a yearlong process to discern the needs of the conference churches in their ministry with older adults. From this process and with the financial support of the Golden Cross Foundation, the advisory team proposed that an intentional ministry, a separate entity from both the Golden Cross Foundation and the Tennessee Conference Committee on Older-Adult Ministries, should be started to provide consultation, training, and support, resources, and networking opportunities for local church leaders desiring to become intentional in ministry by, with, and for older adults. The new ministry would be called "Encore Ministries." The advisory team proposed that a paid part-time staff person should be hired to serve as director for this new ministry. Funding for Encore Ministries would be provided by a grant from the Golden Cross Foundation.

Both the board of directors of the Golden Cross Foundation and the members of the Tennessee Conference Committee on Older-Adult Ministries approved Encore Ministries. A three-year agreement was established, and Encore Ministries became a reality in the fall of 2015.

ENCORE Ministries

The mission of Encore Ministries is to provide consultation, training and support, resource information, and networking opportunities for local church leaders in the Tennessee

Conference in starting and sustaining older-adult ministries. In addition to providing workshops and seminars on older-adult ministries, the director meets with local church leaders and helps them assess the needs and strengths of their congregations related to older-adult ministries. There is no cost to local churches for the services of Encore Ministries.

Along with the part-time director for Encore Ministries, there is an Encore Ministries Advisory Team composed of representatives from both the Golden Cross Foundation and the Tennessee Conference Committee on Older-Adult Ministries. The Encore Ministries Advisory Team oversees the work of the director, provides guidance for this ministry, and evaluates the ministry's effectiveness.

The Tennessee Conference has started a major marketing effort to make local church leaders aware of the work of Encore Ministries. Networking among church leaders is taking place, and Encore Ministries has a website: www.encoretnumc.org. One of the difficulties faced by Encore Ministries is helping church leaders see the need for intentional older-adult ministries. While most of the local churches in the Tennessee Conference are graying congregations, church leaders are generally encouraged to reach young people. With limited time, personnel, and resources, many church leaders lack knowledge and interest in providing intentional ministry by, with and for older adults. Gaining the support and confidence of the conference leadership is important to the overall success of Encore Ministries. Conference leaders, through participation in local charge conferences (local church annual meetings), can encourage local churches that are struggling with ministry issues to seek the guidance and resources of Encore Ministries.

Encore Ministry Leadership Team

Engaging in intentional ministry by, with, and for older adults for a local church can be a complicated and challenging experience. Some local churches may oppose using their leadership and resources for older-adult ministry, even if the church is a graying congregation. The belief that churches should place all their time and effort in reaching families and young people is a strong motivator for ignoring the needs of older adults.

To help local church leaders overcome many of the problems in starting intentional older-adult ministries, Encore Ministries created a team of volunteer leaders. The Encore Ministry Leadership Team, made up of volunteers from the various districts, serve as frontline leaders in supporting older-adult ministries within the district churches. The Encore Ministry Leadership Team members receive regular training and support from the director of Encore Ministries.

Encore Ministry Leadership Team members provide basic consultation for district churches in starting intentional senior-adult ministries. The team members are known in their respective districts, and they have the opportunity—through participation in district meetings and events—to become familiar with local churches and their leaders.

Encore Ministries team leaders provide the following:

1. Advocacy—Team leaders advocate on behalf of the needs of older adults and older-adult concerns in their district churches and local communities.

2. Consultation—Team leaders meet with local church older-adult ministry leadership teams. They work with local church leaders in assessing the church's ministry by, with, and for older adults. They provide information and resources on starting and sustaining older-adult ministries. They assist local church leaders in developing ministry by, with, and for older adults.

3. Training—Team leaders provide training that benefits district churches by supplying current information, building knowledge, and sharing resources in district leadership training events.

4. Networking—Team leaders help establish networks for church leaders in their districts in support of older-adult ministries.

5. Resource Knowledge—Team leaders gather resource information concerning the needs of older adults from the district. This information includes local and state agencies.

6. Network as a Team—Team leaders meet regularly along with the director of Encore Ministries for information sharing, knowledge building, and support. In addition to receiving training and support in understanding ministries by, with, and for older adults, team leaders are guided in ways of consulting with local churches.

Encore Ministry team leaders use a series of questions to prepare for and guide the local church consultation. Encore

Ministry team leaders are encouraged to know the answers to the questions prior to the visit with local churches:

1. *What is the purpose of the visit?* Team leaders recognize that there are different purposes for a visit; therefore, different resources and information will be shared. Before meeting with local church leaders, team leaders know what the local church wants and expects from the visit. They are clear about the location and day and time of the meeting.

2. *What do you already know about the church you are visiting?* Team leaders know whether the church is a large-, medium- or small-membership church. They know if the church is in an urban, suburban, or rural setting and the percentage of older adults in the church. Team leaders know if the pastor is full- or part-time and if the congregation is an older, graying congregation. They also know if there is a senior-adult ministry team already in existence in the church or if a ministry is just starting.

3. *Who will attend the meeting?* Team leaders know whether they are meeting with the pastor and key church leaders or with another set of church leaders. They also know how many people will attend the meeting, so they will have enough resources ready to distribute.

4. *As a team leader, are you prepared for the meeting?* Team leaders know that basic courtesy and respect requires that they are not only on time for the meeting but that they will arrive about thirty minutes prior to

the start of the meeting. Arriving at the church before the start of the meeting allows team leaders time to set up any equipment they need and to visit with people already present for the meeting.

5. *Where will the meeting be held?* Team leaders know the correct address of the local church, parking availability, and the meeting room location. They also know what equipment will be available for their use, such as an LCD projector and screen for PowerPoint presentation, a chalk or dry board (or newsprint and easel) and markers, and a television and DVD player.

6. *What does the meeting space look like?* Team leaders will make sure the lighting, room temperature, and acoustics are conducive for learning. They will place chairs around tables so that participants can engage in conversation with one another and also clearly see the visiting team leader.

7. *What will you do when you start the meeting?* Team leaders will invite the pastor or key local church leader to open with prayer and ask that the pastor or local church leader introduce the team leader to the participants. The team leader will invite participants from the local church to introduce themselves. Team leaders will also explain why they have been invited to attend the meeting and share information about Encore Ministries.

8. *How will you proceed with the meeting?* Team leaders invite participants to share information about their ministry with older adults or ways older adults are involved in the ministry of the church. Team leaders will share

information about intentional ministry by, with, and for senior adults as found in chapters 5, 6 and 7 of this book. Team leaders will share information about developing and conducting an older-adult survey within the church and/or community as found in Appendixes C, D, E, F, and G of this book. Team leaders will share information about their own local church ministry or that of other local churches as resource information for specific ministries with older adults. Team leaders will also share information about grant funding from the Golden Cross Foundation.

9. *Before leaving, are there additional questions or concerns?* Prior to ending the meeting, which in most cases will generally last about two hours, team leaders will ask participants if there are any additional questions or concerns. Team leaders will review with the group any action taken or decisions reached at the meeting. Team leaders will thank the pastor and/or church leadership team for inviting them. Team leaders will inform the group that they will follow up with the pastor or key church leader within the next six weeks.

10. *Will information be recorded for future reference?* Team leaders will indicate when and where the meeting was held, who attended the meeting, any questions or discussion items that need immediate follow-up, and a record of the action or direction the local church will be taking.

Encore Ministries is a unique program that is working successfully in the Tennessee Conference of The United

Methodist Church. Naturally, there are other ways judicatory bodies can relate to local churches in developing ministries by, with, and for older adults. It is clear, however, that every conference or judicatory body should have a committee or task force concerned with ministry and the needs of our aging population.

Conclusion

Older adults deserve respect, dignity, and equal opportunity. Local churches are called to be advocates for older adults, but local churches alone cannot meet all the needs of our aging population. The church must be able to direct older adults, their family members, and caregivers to appropriate resources. Local churches need help. Many church leaders have received little or no training in gerontology or in older-adult ministries. Very few seminaries offer coursework related to our aging population and older-adult ministries. Unless denominations and judicatory bodies assist local church leaders in developing ministries by, with, and for older adults, older adults will likely see the church as merely a club or a fellowship group.

The future of the church will depend on individuals who are spiritually mature. Annual conferences and other judicatory bodies need to advocate for proactive ministries that provide training, support, and resources for local church leaders in their ministry with older adults.

What about your judicatory body, your conference, district, synod, diocese, or presbytery? Is your church taking the necessary steps to be proactive in meeting the needs—spiritual, physical, emotional, mental, and social—of an aging population? Does your church see this as an age of opportunity?

CHAPTER 8

Congregational Care Ministry

"Religion that is pure and undefiled before God, the Father, is this: to care for orphans and widows in their distress..."

—JAMES 1:27

Many congregations have ministries that respond effectively to relatively short-term needs related to brief periods of illness at home, hospitalization, death, or social needs such as food, clothing, transportation, financial assistance, and more. Many also have ministries that respond in varying ways to longer-term challenges, such as visitation of homebound members and nursing home residents.

Few congregations have dedicated ministries with members and neighbors who would benefit from a more comprehensive support ministry that responds to a range or continuum of needs that typically fall outside of existing ministries and continue for prolonged periods of time. And perhaps even fewer congregations have an organized faith community nursing ministry (parish nurse ministry).

In this chapter, we will briefly review four specific areas of congregational care ministry for meeting the needs of older adults and their families: congregational caregiver support group ministry, adult day-care ministry, elder-abuse awareness and response ministry, and United Methodist SAGE Ministry.

Congregational Caregiver Support Group Ministry

While we read and hear much about our aging church and society, it is important to remember that most older adults live independently and are active in their families and communities. Less than five percent of the older-adult population reside in long-term care facilities or nursing homes, and most older people are never institutionalized on a permanent basis. When older adults become frail or dependent, however, family support networks usually provide caregiving.

Family members have traditionally been and continue to be the principal source of service and support for functionally dependent older people, as well as chronically disabled loved ones of any age. Families provide a wide range of assistance, from occasional help with shopping and transportation to financial assistance to primary in-home caregiving. Wives and daughters most often fill the caregiver role, but husbands, sons, and other family members and friends also frequently care for frail or dependent older adults.

This help is not without its price, however. Caregivers can experience weariness and often feel discouraged from the lack of emotional support and the difficulty of finding needed help. Many caregivers are unaware of available resources for assistance. While some caregivers seldom leave the house for relaxation or respite, others are busy juggling family, work, and personal needs. Even the most loving caregiver is likely to experience stress, fatigue, and anger.

Caregiving for a family member can be very rewarding, but it is also hard work; and caregivers are often filled with conflicting emotions. Caregiving often means sacrificing one's own pastimes and plans for the good of someone else. Women, especially, who provide long-term care for a chronically ill loved one often suffer serious long-term financial consequences—including reduced Social Security, pension, and retirement income—as a result of reduced time in the workforce.

Even worse, perhaps, is the physical and emotional toll of extended caregiving. Family caregivers are more likely to experience negative health effects such as anxiety, depression, and chronic disease. As overworked and underappreciated as family caregivers are, health systems, under pressure to reduce costs, increasingly rely on them to manage illness at home.

Caregivers often have difficulty finding personal time, balancing work and family responsibilities, and managing their emotional and physical stress. Five of the most important needs for caregivers are reliable information, helpful resources, available services, caring assistance, and emotional support.

The church can and should take necessary steps to help family caregivers as they provide support for loved ones. One important approach for churches to take is to establish a caregiver support group. By participating in a caregiver support group, family members can experience numerous benefits:

- First, the caregiver's feelings of loneliness and isolation are reduced in the nonjudgmental company of others facing similar situations.
- Second, the caregiver receives information about the aging process and about available community resources.
- Third, interaction among caregivers with similar problems and concerns helps develop skills in stress management, problem solving, communication, and home-care techniques.
- Fourth, group participation builds a support network that may well carry over beyond group meetings into lasting friendships.
- Fifth, and finally, opportunities for the spiritual growth of both the caregiver and the frail or dependent family member can be enhanced.

As a church leader, when starting a caregiver support group, you will want to become knowledgeable about community resources. Although communities differ in the types and number of resources they offer, certain core services supported by government funding, private funding, or business enterprises are available in most areas. You will want to contact the social services department of your local hospital or other health-care facility. Also, many nursing homes and other long-term care facilities have social workers on staff. Social workers and geriatric case managers can be helpful in providing important information about the availability of local resources. In addition, contact your local area agency on aging office. The staff of this agency know many of the services already being provided in the community.

In providing support for adult children of aging parents or offering a seminar or program on caregiving, never use the phrase "parenting your parents" to describe the role of family caregivers. Adult children never become their parents' parents. There is no such thing as a second childhood. Adult children do not become "parents of their parents." This is demeaning and offensive language, and it is not a biblical description of the role of adult children in providing care for their aging parents. As Jesus was hanging on the cross, we read in Scripture: "When Jesus saw his mother and the disciple whom he loved standing beside her, he said to his mother, 'Woman, here is your son.' Then he said to the disciple, 'Here is your mother.' And from that hour the disciple took her into his own home" (John 19:26-27). Jesus did not say, "John, in my absence, you will now need to parent my mother." Rather, Jesus spoke to John, indicating that he was to care for his mother.

When aging parents have difficulties with activities of daily living, dementia, or very serious illness, there are certainly new responsibilities and a change in roles between aging parents and adult children, but adult children don't parent their parents, even in the most extreme cases. Rather, adult children become their parents' caregivers. Adult children help manage their parents' care and well-being. But, they never, ever become their "parents' parents."

Church leaders can help adult children by reminding them that aging parents, whatever their problems or disabilities may be, are not children. Their parents are, and always will be, their parents, and they will always be their children. The Bible speaks of honoring and respecting our parents. When the church provides programs with the title, "Parenting Your Parents," we are not giving aging parents the respect they deserve. Older adults must be treated with dignity, honesty, and respect. To do otherwise is demeaning for older adults. Trusting them to handle their own choices or problems is often a great measure of loving concern, more so than taking care of the problem for them. Think about it: Would you want your children to parent you? Of course not. But, you would want your adult children to help care for your needs, to respect your decisions, and to help manage your health and well-being, if necessary.

Provide respite-care services for caregivers. Encourage family members to share in caregiving responsibilities and invite other church members to become involved. Establish support group meeting times and places convenient for all participants. And remember that when you conduct your support group, you will need to have a ministry available for the care-receiver. It may be necessary that you have volunteer teams visiting with the care-receivers while the caregivers participate in the support group. Or, you might hold the support group gathering during a period of time when the care-receiver is participating in the adult day-care ministry.

By creating caregiver support groups in your congregation, you can help primary caregivers provide vital and loving care for frail and dependent older adults or for chronically disabled people of any age.

Adult Day-Care Ministry

Caregivers need support and routine breaks from caregiving. Occasionally, all caregivers feel frustration, guilt, fatigue, and isolation. Because of the many and variable tasks of caregiving, many caregivers find it difficult to take a break.

In the past, many churches started child care and preschool programs to serve the needs of a growing population of children. With the increase in numbers of older adults in our churches and communities, and the desire of more people to continue living in their own homes, local congregations are beginning to address the question of church-sponsored adult day-care ministry.

There is a growing need for churches to provide a safe place for older adults who need special attention and care so that families who are providing care will have some free time each week. Families who face the pressures that come from constant care with an older adult who is experiencing the initial stages of dementia and memory loss will find that respite is well-deserved time off.

Establishing an adult day-care ministry is an opportunity for community ministry by a local church. Volunteers, oftentimes older adults themselves, could provide this service on a half-day or full-day basis, and from one day to several times a week. The purpose of adult day-care ministry is to provide social interaction, stimulation, and friendship in a caring, safe environment for those experiencing early stages of memory loss, as well as to provide respite for the caregivers. Adult day-care ministry provides services to promote social, physical, and emotional well-being for older adults. Some churches call this ministry the Sunny Day Club.

Services some adult day-care ministries offer include: snacks and/or meals; structured opportunities for recreational activities, such as arts and crafts, music therapy and exercises. Additional activities may include reading the newspaper or using the computer for internet resources, watching television or DVD programs, playing board games, Bible study, and other learning activities.

If no medication or physical therapy is administered and no meals are provided, an adult day ministry may not require state licensing. However, before beginning an adult day ministry, contact your state agency and carefully review the rules and regulations.

Churches' multipurpose rooms on the ground level with easy access to a parking lot, secure entrances, and accessible restrooms close to the room are ideal for this particular ministry. Having a church kitchen nearby makes snack preparation easy. A snack or light meal may be provided by the church or brought from home. It is important that participants are able to get around fairly well on their own.

Having a one-to-one ratio of volunteers to participants will be needed at first for ministry with each older person. The adjustments to a change in routine and breaking the habit of always having a family member on call will require time and patience. Make certain that staff and volunteers are trained in first aid and CPR, and have background checks for all volunteers to ensure a safe environment. Family members can help with transportation, wheelchairs, and understanding personal idiosyncrasies of the individual older adults.

An adult day ministry is one means of helping caregivers in a community. Unfortunately, when stress and anxiety become too great for caregivers, elder abuse is more likely to take place.

Elder Abuse Awareness and Response Ministry

In a society that does not value aging and growing older, people can become indifferent to the needs and well-being of its older members. As the older-adult population has grown steadily in numbers over the years, the incidences of elder-abuse perpetrated against them have also grown. When older adults become dependent on someone else to care for their needs and to perform basic tasks that they can no longer do for themselves, they become vulnerable to occurrences of elder abuse.

Every day, headlines throughout the United States paint a grim picture of older adults who have been abused, neglected, and exploited, often by the people they trust most. The great majority of abusers are family members, most often an adult child or spouse. But other abusers may include other family and old friends, newly developed "friends" who intentionally prey on older adults, and professionals and service providers in positions of trust.

Elder abuse is often described as any knowing, intended, or careless act that causes harm or serious risk of harm to an older person. Recognition of and mechanisms for dealing with elder abuse are far behind strides that have been made in child abuse awareness and protection. While there is currently no federal law protecting elders from abuse, all fifty states have adopted laws specifically dealing with elder abuse, neglect, and exploitation. Laws and definitions of terms vary considerably from one state to another, but broadly defined, abuse may be:

- *Physical abuse*: use of force to threaten or physically cause pain or injury to a vulnerable older person
- *Emotional abuse*: verbal or nonverbal attacks, threats, rejection, isolation, or belittling acts that could cause mental anguish, pain, or distress
- *Sexual abuse*: sexual contact that is forced, tricked, threatened, or coerced upon an older person
- *Financial abuse*: the illegal taking, misuse, or concealment of funds, property, or assets of a vulnerable older adult
- *Neglect*: a caregiver's failure or refusal to provide food, shelter, health care, protection, or safety for an older adult
- *Abandonment*: Desertion of a frail or vulnerable older adult by anyone with a duty of care
- *Self-neglect*: An inability to understand the consequences of one's own actions or inaction, which leads to harm or endangerment.

Another type of abuse, not part of any state or federal law that defines elder abuse, but one that greatly concerns the church and church leaders is *spiritual neglect*. Spiritual neglect is the failure of congregations and church leaders to provide for the spiritual well-being of older members. Spiritual neglect generally takes place with older adults who are homebound or home-centered, or who reside in nursing homes or assisted living facilities. When clergy or church leaders fail to provide for the spiritual support and faith development of vulnerable older adults (including visitation, administration of the Sacrament of Eucharist or Holy Communion, prayer and devotional reading, etc.) on a regular basis for members who no longer are able to attend regular worship services and study classes, spiritual abuse or neglect becomes a reality.

Elder abuse can occur anywhere—in the home, in nursing homes or other institutions, and sadly, even in church settings. Elder abuse can happen to anyone. It affects older adults of all socioeconomic groups, religions, cultures, and races; however, women and frail older adults are more likely to be victimized.

Unfortunately, abusers are not always easy to spot. Adding to the problem, victims may not be physically or mentally able to report their abuse, or they may be isolated and too afraid or ashamed to tell someone. While there is no typical profile of an abuser, the following are some behavioral signs that may indicate problems:

- Unusual degree of fear or submissiveness to caregiver
- Isolation from family, friends, and community

- Home environment concerns, such as: clutter in the house, foul smells, and disheveled appearance
- Physical injuries, such as bruises, broken bones, and burns and repeated "accidental" injuries
- Characterizes a loved one as *"Dr. Jekyll and Mr. Hyde"*
- Says or hints at being afraid or "walking on eggshells" at home
- Makes veiled disclosures, such as *"My daughter has a temper,"* or *"I have to ask my son's permission for everything."*

Church leaders need to be aware of elder abuse because they may be the first stop for help. The pastor, Sunday school teacher, or other key church figure may be the only person (except the abuser) in the victim's life. By knowing the warning signs of elder abuse, church leaders will be better prepared to help and may save a life. In many states, there is mandatory reporting of elder abuse by all professionals, including clergy.

If the victim reaches out to you as a leader in the faith community, you should listen with compassion and without judgment. Be available to learn more fully about the situation from the victim. Offer spiritual and other needed forms of support and help. Reassure the victim of elder abuse that the congregation is with her or him during this crisis, that he or she is not alone, and that you are supportive and will help.

Keep in mind that immediate resources might be needed for the victim, including temporary caregivers or temporary housing. Emergency funds may be needed for food, rent or mortgage payments, transportation, utilities, new locks to secure victims' homes, repairs, relocation costs, respite care, home modification, and legal fees. Shelter may be needed for various reasons. Older victims of domestic violence may need a safe haven from batterers. Victims of financial abuse may need temporary housing if they have been evicted from their homes as a result of abuse. Others may need shelter because they have been abandoned by their caregivers or if caregivers have been terminated or arrested.

If you suspect elder abuse and have not been informed by the victim, you will need to take action. Always put the safety of the victim first. Look for indicators of abuse. If possible, gently ask questions and talk with the abused person. Check with others to see if they have noticed changes in the situation surrounding the vulnerable older adult and confer with other professionals, if possible. Consider strategies to break the isolation of the vulnerable older adult such as inviting the person to an activity or program. Suggest visiting the older adult in the home. Focus on the strengths, resiliency, and natural allies of the older person.

Every state and most counties have an agency or adult protective services that is responsible for responding to elder abuse. To find out where to report elder abuse, call the Eldercare Locator at 1-800-677-1116 or to find your state's number, go to the elder abuse website at www.elderabuse-center.org and then click "Where to Report Abuse." If you are concerned about a nursing home or assisted living facility resident, the long-term care ombudsman also can serve as a resource. To find your local long-term care ombudsman's office, call the U.S. Administration on Aging's Eldercare Locator at 1-800-677-1116. If someone is in immediate danger, call 911 or your local police. You do not need to prove abuse to make a report.

Congregations can take appropriate action to help prevent elder abuse. Church leaders should:

- educate themselves and other church members about elder abuse.
- create a safe place for older adults by making the church a place where elderly victims can come for help.
- educate the congregation on the subject of violence against and abuse of elders.
- give sermons and prepare newsletter and website articles that inform the congregation about elder abuse.
- inform older adults and their families about various frauds and scams that may be happening in your area or across the nation.
- support the family caregiver through the various ministries of the church, such as a caregiver support group, an adult day-care ministry, or financial assistance if needed, and by encouraging the caregiver to take care of himself/herself by getting respite.
- establish a **friendly visitor program** where teams of two members each from your congregation regularly visit homebound and home-centered members, as well as people living in nursing homes and assisted living facilities.
- start a faith community nursing ministry (parish nurse ministry) in which a knowledgeable and professional health-care worker can help educate the congregation as well as be an observer of the needs of homebound

members. For more information on faith community nursing ministry, visit www.westberginstitute.org or www.churchhealth.org.

United Methodist SAGE Ministry

Older adulthood has the potential to become the best stage of life, an age of liberation when adults combine newfound freedoms with prolonged health. It can be a time when individuals make their most important contributions to life, faith, society, and the world. As in all stages of personal and spiritual development, aging encompasses special tasks; one such task is the desire to give back and to help benefit succeeding generations. (Erik Erikson suggested this developmental stage is "generativity versus stagnation."[1])

If, in fact, as we age we have the opportunity to grow in wisdom, to gain experience, and to deepen our faith, to what end or purpose does all this have? Is it beneficial for Christians to watch forty-eight hours of television seven days a week or to play eighteen holes of golf, five days a week? There isn't necessarily anything wrong with watching television or playing golf, but if people are living longer and are healthier than were previous generations, what purpose does living longer have for individuals and for our world?

Perhaps it's time for congregations to invite senior adults to really put faith into practice by creating intentional opportunities for older adults to live out their Christian discipleship in service to others. Congregations could start a United Methodist SAGE Ministry, and members of this ministry would be "Sages." SAGE (Senior Advocate, Gifted and Empowered) Ministry would be more than a fellowship or an "eatin' & meetin'" program. Sages would model Christian "elderhood" in our world today. Rather than thinking of old age as a vast wasteland, Sages would be engaged in serving Christ in all things and with all people. At the heart of their service, Sages will faithfully adhere to the Great Commandment which is "you shall love the Lord your God with all your heart, and with all your soul, and with all your mind, and with all your strength, (*and*) you shall love your neighbor as yourself" (Mark 12:30-31).

What would it mean for the revitalization of our churches if we started a SAGE Ministry with older adults? If we as Christians were to mobilize our older men and women to confront the ills of our society and send them out in pairs like the original disciples, we could change the face of this land. In this age of opportunity, Sages could make a significant difference in the lives of not only older adults, but in the lives of people of all ages, their families, and their communities.

Guiding Principles of the SAGE Ministry

Name: The United Methodist SAGE Ministry name is a deliberate attempt to avoid any name associated with age and to honor the sturdy, widely possessed, unintimidating assets present in many older adults: faith, wisdom, and experience. The acronym SAGE stands for Senior Advocate, Gifted and Empowered.

SAGE ministry members should engage problems of major significance in the community and world. Older adults, growing in faith and spiritual maturity, would be involved in advocacy for all God's children at every age and stage of life. Older adults, invited to grow as disciples of Jesus Christ, would be empowered to make a difference in the lives of individuals, communities, and the world. SAGE ministry members would be caregivers of people and stewards of God's creation.

Service: SAGE ministry members (Sages) would serve as senior life guides, older adults who walk alongside others and share their presence, prayers, experience, and wisdom. They may provide practical help and advice, resource information, and knowledge that affects the well-being of others.

Commitment: Joining the SAGE ministry requires a major commitment for older adults for a defined period of time. For some people, the commitment is to become involved in community service projects for a lengthy period of time. For others, the commitment is for a shorter duration in various parts of the world. Many older adults are involved in wonderful mission work around the world and in various regions of the country. Often, however, mission and service opportunities can also be met in an individual's local community.

Deployment: Sages may be deployed in sufficient concentration to be a presence wherever they serve, whether locally, regionally, or throughout the world. Teams may be created for mutual support, encouragement, and experience.

Leadership: Sages provide initiative, creativity, and leadership. Leaders would be named by the church council and selected by the members. Leadership needs would depend upon the specific mission and service involvement and the duration of the specific ministry.

Spiritual Growth and Learning: Members of the SAGE ministry would engage in advocacy on behalf of older adults; practice spiritual disciplines (prayer, Bible study, worship, Communion, fasting, etc.); and be engaged in acquiring new experiences and gaining new knowledge.

Recognizing that many older adults are already involved as Christian disciples helping to meet the needs of children, youth, and adults in their communities and throughout the world, SAGE ministry can be a creative way of putting faith into practice in an intentional, comprehensive ministry. SAGE ministry can be a critical venture for revitalizing congregations and communities. SAGE ministry can be adapted and designed to meet the needs of various levels of skills and abilities of older adults on the local level, as well as encouraging their participation in such endeavors as global missions.

What is the purpose of living longer if it is not to fulfill the purpose of God? SAGE ministry is a way of inviting older adults to engage in spiritual growth and of organizing older adults to be in service to others. SAGE ministry engages older adults in Christian discipleship. Through this model of Christian elderhood, older adults have an opportunity to find meaning and purpose in the later years. They will experience the reality of the psalmist's yearning by "proclaiming God's might to all the generations."

Conclusion

Our society lacks an effective system to address caregiving. Given America's refusal as a "developed" nation to have a universal health-care system, there is no wonder we lack effective caregiving support. As a result, caregivers—the majority of whom are women—are often pushed beyond their means and suffer long-term consequences as they struggle to meet the caregiving needs of those who depend on them.

Until a crisis occurs, many congregations do not give much thought to the needs of older adults or their caregivers or to developing a congregational care ministry. Older adults are often taken for granted. They are present in worship, providing leadership in the church, giving financially to its ministry, and engaged in mission and service opportunities. But with increasing longevity, growing numbers of older adults with chronic illnesses, and more older adults living alone, the need for congregational care ministry will become more important. With decreasing federal and state dollars, shrinking governmental programs that support the needs of older adults and their caregivers, and with society's challenge to provide effective quality health care, churches are faced with new and challenging opportunities for helping both care-receivers and caregivers.

Although more people than ever before will experience an extended phase of life, this does not mean that people will age without limitations or disabilities. In fact, in our culture, those who are less fortunate because of chronic health conditions or disability and meager financial resources run the risk of being deprived of the necessary care and dignity. But, living longer should not mean unnecessary hardship. Congregational care ministry is the context in which the church's values and faith are transmitted and the will of God is realized.

This is an age of opportunity for many churches. The need is now, and the needs of older adults and their families are growing. Congregations that provide intentional congregational care and that fully include older adults in this vital ministry will witness God's love for all people to the whole community.

CHAPTER 9

Additional Ideas for Intentional Ministry

"For old age is not honored for length of time, or measured by number of years; but understanding is gray hair for anyone, and a blameless life is ripe old age."
—Wisdom of Solomon 4:8-9, Apocrypha

As you begin developing intentional ministry by, with, and for older adults, use the following suggestions to help guide your leadership in planning.

1. Initially and continuously, use older adults in your planning process. If possible, develop a committee or team for older-adult ministries and listen to the needs and suggestions of older people in your faith community.

2. Continue to study the needs of older adults. Familiarize yourself with aging concerns. Be sure you know whom you are trying to reach and why.

3. Remember that older adults are all different. Provide a variety of different activities and programs to reach as many older adults as possible. Younger older adults (boomers) may not want to do the same activities as older older adults. Also, older women may want to do different activities than older men do. Recognize that married couples may want to engage in ministries different from those enjoyed by single or widowed adults. Be sensitive to these differences.

4. Find out what activities older adults want to participate in. Conduct a survey to secure the necessary information.

5. Do some networking. Look for people or programs already providing services to older adults. Get input from these sources.

6. Develop programs that meet the needs of various older adults. Be sure to include both structured and unstructured activities. You do not have to fill every waking moment with a program.

7. Coordinate planning and carry out a variety of activities for older-adult participants. Make sure all facilities are accessible and restrooms are located nearby.

8. If appropriate, obtain from each older-adult participant basic health information, including diet restrictions, medication, physicians' and family members' phone numbers, and any activity constraints.

9. Meet on a regular basis for assessing needs, providing information from reports, planning programs, evaluating existing and ongoing projects.
10. Keep informed about issues and concerns relating to older adults.

As you plan for intentional older-adult ministry, keep in mind that every older adult is a unique individual and one ministry idea does not meet all needs. Be sure to identify needs and plan ministry accordingly. Listed below are just some of the many ideas or "best practices" for creating intentional ministry by, with, and for older adults:

Accessibility Teams: Invite retired builders, people with handicapping conditions, and older adults to form an accessibility team. The task of the team is to identify problem areas in the church and on the grounds that make it difficult, hazardous, or unsafe for children, older adults, and people with handicapping conditions.

Advocacy Teams: Invite older adults to form advocacy teams for the purpose of advocating on behalf of the needs and concerns of older adults, including political issues, consumer concerns, health care, violence, and crime. Advocacy teams provide information and insight for the whole congregation.

Advertise Your Older-Adult Ministry: Let everyone in the community know about your older-adult ministry by marketing your program and advertising in local theaters and restaurants, senior citizen centers, ball parks, and other places older adults congregate. If you live in a community where retirees are relocating, market your ministry through the newspaper, online, and in specialty local magazines to reach new people moving into the area.

Book Club: Many older adults enjoy reading and engaging in conversation with others around various books, authors, and topics. Start a book club that reaches older adults. Such a program can be held onsite or online.

C.O.A.P.—Children of Aging Parents: Provide support, networking opportunities, and resource information for adult children of aging parents. Hold seminars and workshops on various topics related to aging: legal concerns, health issues, caregiving resources, and so on.

Make Sure the Church Website Includes Older-Adult Ministry: Review your church website. Do you see photos of older adults on the masthead? Are photos of older adults engaged in worship, study and learning, and service being displayed? Does the church website include a listing of the many activities of older adults? Many older adults use the internet to find resource information and, if new to the area, may look at the church website to see what ministries are available for older adults. Make certain your church website includes older adults as well as people of all ages.

Companion Services: Some older adults, particularly people with mobility issues, may need a bit of help when they visit the doctor, dentist, pharmacy, grocery store, and so on. A ministry of companion services, provides teams of two to serve as companions and assist older people in their scheduled appointments by going along with them.

Evangelism Teams: Train and empower older adults for witnessing their faith in the saving grace of Jesus Christ with other older adults and with people of all ages. While older adults may have a lifetime of experience in the Christian faith, they may feel uncomfortable about sharing their faith journey and God's love with others. Providing training, support, and resources in evangelism for older adults is important for the church's efforts to reach nonmembers and nonbelievers.

Exercise and Fitness Classes: Regular exercise is important for maintaining health. The church could provide opportunities for older adults to participate in low-impact aerobics classes, yoga classes, or other forms of exercise designed for older adults. Contact your local YMCA/YWCA to ask for an instructor to lead these sessions in your church fellowship hall or Christian life building.

Faith Community Nursing Ministry (Parish Nurse Ministry): Faith community nursing ministry, commonly known as parish nursing, promotes health and wellness in the local congregation and more broadly throughout the surrounding community. Faith community nursing is the specialized practice of professional nursing that focuses on the intentional care of the spirit as part of the process of promoting holistic health while preventing or minimizing illness in a faith community.

Field Trips: Learning makes aging more fun. Include ministry opportunities for older adults to engage in educational, informational, and recreational travel. Plan one-day outings or several-day and overnight travels.

Flowers for Homebound and Nursing Home Residents: Following worship services, if you use fresh flowers on the church altar, take the flowers as a gift to homebound and nursing home residents.

Fraud and Scam Awareness: Through the AARP Fraud Watch program or other fraud and scam awareness sources, regularly post information about the frauds and scams taking place in your area in your church newsletter, worship bulletin, or on your church website to help keep older adults safe.

Game Day: Once a week or monthly, hold a game day in your church for older adults. (Include games that involve mental stimulation.) You might invite older adults to play Bridge, Bingo, or various board games.

Grand Friends: With today's mobility among family members, some older adults may not have grandchildren, or their grandchildren may live at a distance and rarely have an opportunity to be with their grandparents. Grand Friends Ministry provides an opportunity for older adults to share their love and knowledge as "surrogate grandparents" with children and youth who have few or no extended family members living in the community.

Health Fair and Screening Day: Invite older adults to participate in a senior health fair and screening. Involve medical and health-care personnel from the community and provide blood pressure checks and minor exams.

Health-care Equipment Loan Ministry: Collect and store, clean, and distribute health-care equipment to people in need. Equipment for loan might include: canes, walkers, wheelchairs, and potty chairs.

Helping Hands: Older adults want to serve the needs of others. Invite older adults to help start and manage a church food ministry and clothing pantry for people in need.

Home Maintenance and Minor Home Repair Teams: Some older adults find it difficult to remain in their homes simply because of minor home maintenance needs. Older adults with skills can help others stay in their homes as long as possible by painting, changing light bulbs, mowing grass, doing minor carpentry, and doing laundry and other home chores.

Homebound Sunday School Class: On Sunday mornings, gather a class of older adults around a table in a classroom setting. In the middle of the table, put a speaker phone and invite homebound class members to participate in the class learning and discussion by using the speaker phone. Another method for tech–savvy seniors is to use Skype or some other internet program that will allow homebound members to participate in the classroom from an offsite location.

Homebound Worship Participation: Similar to the homebound Sunday school class, this ministry invites homebound members to read Scripture, offer the morning prayer, or participate in other liturgy acts by using their telephones and having their voices sent through the church sound system. This ministry may also use video technology. Or prepare a DVD in advance to show during worship. Using Skype is also an option for worship.

House Sharing: If your church is in a college community, you might start a house sharing ministry with older adults and college students. Older adults could share housing with college students in exchange for chore service, minor home repair, cooking, and laundry.

Intergenerational Retreat: Invite older adults and youth to participate in an overnight retreat together. Using a church campground with accessible facilities, plan for games, meals, Bible study, and sharing together. Make this a fun learning experience for everyone.

Kitchen Band: Invite older adults to make musical instruments from household and other common materials, such as pots and pans, old washboards, kazoos, and so on. Enjoy performing at nursing homes, retirement communities, and church functions.

Latch-Key Kid Ministry: If your church is located near an elementary school, invite older adults to provide an afterschool program as a safe place for the children who live nearby. The program may be for one hour or longer and is a helpful ministry for children until their parents return home from work. Include tutoring and mentoring opportunities for children.

Library with Resources on Aging Concerns: Place in your church library reading materials, including audio and large-print books, that are suitable for older adults. Make sure your library also includes resources and information about caregiving, aging health concerns, area senior services directory, and government programs that have an impact on aging concerns.

Life Review Class: Invite older adults to participate in life review and reminiscence classes. Engage older adults in a program that not only provides opportunities for reviewing the past experiences of their lives but also invites them to gain insight into what God may be calling them to in the future.

Living History Recorded: Older adults have had unique and varied life experiences. Inviting older adults to share their life journeys and faith stories is a wonderful learning experience for the older adults and for younger people.. Living histories may be recorded on DVD, in writing, and/or orally in worship and Sunday school classes.

Lunch Partners: Living alone for many older adults can generate feelings of isolation and loneliness. Invite volunteer older adults to eat a meal once a week with a homebound member in his or her home.

Marriage Enrichment Classes/Retreat: We often think of marriage enrichment as a ministry for young couples. However, older adults who have been married for many years and are now retired and living together twenty-four hours a day may need to develop new communication skills. Older married couples should be invited to participate in marriage enrichment classes or a retreat. Such a ministry may be designed specifically for older couples, or there may be programs that are intergenerational and involve young couples as well.

Meals: Older adults participate in opportunities for sharing meals with others on a regular basis. This ministry might include a program that provides meals for needy seniors, for homebound people (such as meals-on-wheels), and for people following hospitalization.

Mentoring and Tutoring: Invite older adults to serve as mentors for children, youth, and other adults. Engage older adults in ministering with children in vacation Bible school programs, with youth during confirmation classes, and with adults who are new to the church and/or considering church membership.

Ministry with LGBT Older Adults: Many LGBT older adults often feel isolated and alone. LGBT older adults, no less than others, need opportunities to grow in faith and to gain a deeper relationship with God through the saving grace of Jesus Christ. Congregations that welcome and fully include LGBT older adults will witness to God's love for all people in the whole community.

Mission Opportunities: Invite older adults to participate on mission trips (both regionally and globally) and to serve local community needs through mission opportunities. Such activities might include a local Habitat for Humanity project, a Volunteer in Mission activity, or a NOMAD (RVer's who travel together throughout the year and work on various mission projects across the country) project.

Monthly Luncheon and Meeting Program: Older adults join together each month for a shared community meal and enjoy a program presentation. The program presentation may be entertainment, inspirational, and/or informational.

Multigenerational Study Groups: During the summer months, invite people of all ages to study together during the Sunday school hour. Another good time for a multigenerational study group is during special church seasons such as Advent or Lent. Include children, youth, and adults in this ministry along with older adults. Make this experience one that is fun and inspirational for all ages. This might include Bible topics and/or current events.

Nursing Home Sunday School Class and/or Worship Service: Start a Sunday school class and/or regular worship service with residents in a nursing home or an assisted living setting. Involve older adults in planning and leading this ministry.

Older-Adult Choir: Invite older adults to form a special choir. Sing at church, nursing homes, retirement communities, and for the homebound. Plan special events such as Christmas caroling throughout the community.

Older-Adult Printed Newsletter and/or Webpage: Create a printed newsletter or webpage especially for the older adults in your congregation. Invite older adults to submit articles and include announcements about church meetings and activities. Also provide information about community activities and agency services specifically designed for older adults.

Pet Ministry: Many older adults love dogs, cats, and other small animals, yet are unable to care for them. This ministry shares the love of gentle animals with older adults. Pets may be taken to visit the homebound and residents in nursing homes and assisted living settings.

Ramp Ministry Teams: Older adults with carpentry skills or "handyperson" talent would build ramps at the homes of people needing ramps constructed for entering and leaving the house.

Recognition Service and Dinner: The congregation sponsors a special dinner, worship service, or other celebration to honor the faith, wisdom, experience, and service of older adults. Both the U.S. Administration on Aging and The United Methodist Church designate the month of May as a special time to recognize older adults.

Respite Fund Ministry: Caregiving expenses can put a great strain on the financial resources of many older adults and families. Start a fund from which families can draw money to pay for respite care or for other caregiving needs.

Retired Men's Breakfast Fellowship: Invite retired men to join together weekly for a breakfast fellowship. Join together for prayer and sharing joys and concerns and include a Bible study or other inspirational reading during the time of fellowship.

Ritual for Older Adults Moving from Their Homes: Invite a small group of older adults to visit an older adult who is moving from his or her home to a nursing home or assisted living setting. During the visit, join together in prayer, Scripture, song, Holy Communion, and words of remembrance and thanksgiving for the years spent in the home. A few months following the move, invite the same small group of older adults to visit the older adult in his or her new home, along with new friends from the facility. Again, join together in prayer, Scripture reading, song, Holy Communion, and words of blessing for living in the new home.

Senior-Adult Yearbook: Invite older adults to create an annual yearbook, and include photos and pictures of activities throughout the year. This is especially helpful for congregations in areas with lots of "snowbirds" (people from the north who visit areas of the south during the winter months) and other older adults who participate in the life of a congregation for a limited time each year.

Senior Bulletin Board: Place a large bulletin board in a strategic location where older adults congregate in the church. Post announcements about events, job opportunities, and photos of recent activities and events on the bulletin board. Change themes regularly and make the postings large and bright for all ages to see.

Senior Crisis Teams: Older adults from a variety of professional areas may form crisis teams to respond to varied personal needs. Team members could be grouped under specific areas of ministry such as money matters, suicide, sudden death of spouse, new widows, legal issues, and health concerns.

Senior Devotional Booklet: Create a devotional resource for older adults and/or people of all ages. Invite older adults to compile a devotional book of Scripture readings, meditations, and prayers for congregational use. Use the devotional book during special church seasons such as Advent or Lent.

Senior Life Guides: People always need help with something, whether it's older adults who want assistance with transportation or household services, or who need advice about raising their grandchildren, gardening, pets, or finances. Train older adults to become senior life guides who can assist other older adults with functional, transportation, social, and safety needs.

Senior Picnic: Invite older adults to enjoy the outdoors by going on a picnic. Include food and drinks, singing, brief meditation on God's creation, hiking, and other nature adventures during the day.

Senior Technology Training Ministry: Invite young people to engage with older adults in the use of technology and to help strengthen the competence of senior adults to participate in and contribute to today's digital culture. By teaching older adults how to use everyday technology such as the internet, smartphones, and tablets, senior technology training ministry can bridge a generational divide and improve older adults' abilities to live independently within our connected society.

Senior Theater: Some older adults enjoy performing before an audience. Start your own faith-based community theater. Invite older adults to practice and perform skits and plays for the church and community.

Service Provider Referral List: Older-adult ministry should include a preferred referral list of service providers in the community. This is a particularly helpful ministry in an area where new retirees are moving or where there are many widows and widowers. Uncertainly about service providers may lead older adults to make bad choices. Congregations should know various service providers in their community and have a list available for older adults so people know where they can receive honest and trustworthy service.

Skype Services: Older adults, including baby boomers, are becoming increasingly tech savvy. Using Skype or other internet services for people who travel and are away from the church for a short or an extended duration can be helpful for people to receive information and to participate in worship, Sunday school, or other study classes.

Social Networking with Seniors: Many older adults are engaged in various forms of social networking on the internet.

Start a blog, Facebook page, or other social networking activity with older adults.

Sunday Afternoon Worship for Homebound: Monthly, quarterly, or at least twice a year, provide a special Sunday afternoon worship service in your church for homebound members and include, if possible, members who reside in nursing homes and assisted living facilities. The service should last no longer than thirty to thirty-five minutes and include a few "old" hymns, a brief meditation and Scripture reading, choir anthem, prayers, and the Eucharist (Holy Communion). It is helpful to select certain times of the year when your church sanctuary may be decorated for a particular season such as Christmas and Easter. You might also include an informal refreshment time following the worship service.

Sunday Morning Respite Care Ministry: Train teams of volunteers to provide respite care on Sunday mornings for homebound seniors so the primary care provider can attend Sunday morning worship services. Teams of two people will spend the hour or two in the home of the home-centered older adult while the caregiver is able to participate in worship and Sunday school.

Telephone Reassurance: A ministry that is particularly helpful for older adults who live alone is a telephone call each day by someone from the church checking on them. Older adults make daily telephone calls to homebound or home-centered members.

Transportation Ministry: A church bus or van may be useful for transporting older adults to the church. If there is not a church vehicle available, older adults and/or other church members can provide transportation for seniors to attend worship and other congregational activities. A full-scale transportation ministry by the church will include transporting older adults to other places throughout the week besides to church, including doctor and dentist visits, pharmacy, grocery store, senior citizen center, community activities, and events.

Ventures in Learning Classes: Keeping the brain sharp and learning new things is important for successful aging. Some churches have started programs sometimes called "Ventures in Learning" that provide educational opportunities for older adults. The classes may be held for one or two hours a week and continue for a set number of weeks. Classes may include topics in such areas as arts and crafts, poetry, literature, history, geography, science, and music. Instructors are usually older adults who are retired or still engaged in a particular area of expertise.

Visitation Ministry Teams: Older adults are trained and form teams of two to visit other older adults who are homebound, lonely, hospitalized, institutionalized, and dying. Visits involve active listening on the part of the visitors, and making faith studies and spiritual traditions (e.g., Holy Communion) available to the homebound.

Weekday Bible Study: Invite older adults in your church and from your community to participate in a weekday Bible study. Include refreshments, sharing joys and concerns, singing, and prayers.

Widow/Widower Support Group Ministry: Churches organize support groups for widows and widowers and engage in intentional ministries with people who are widowed.

Writing Letters and Sending Cards Ministry: Older adults can be invited to write personal letters and to send birthday, anniversary, and special remembrance cards to others. Sending cards to overseas military service personnel, to college students who are away from home, and to people in the mission fields can be an excellent way for your congregation to let people know they are being prayed for and are not forgotten.

CHAPTER 10

Trends in Aging

"Is wisdom with the aged, and understanding in length of days?"

—JOB 12:12

The aging of the U.S. population has wide-ranging implications for our congregations. As we begin to ascertain this age of opportunity for ministry, we need to identify some of the trends that will be the result of this demographic reality. But I hazard only guesses. Just as no one could have foreseen the tragic events of 9/11 or its effects on our nation, or the harsh financial realities of the Great Recession (2008–2011) for many people, there are any number of possible exceptions to the trends I present below and any number of additional trends. I share these insights knowing that in a few years, additional changes and new trends could be added. But, for now, these are the trends I see related to aging in our communities and our congregations.

Trend 1—More Older Adults. In 1900 there were only 3.1 million people in the U.S. who were sixty five years of age or older (one in twenty-five). By 2000 that number had increased to 35 million (one in eight); and by 2030, it is projected that there will be more than 72 million people 65 years of age or older (one in five). An increase in our aging population can be attributed to low infant mortality, lower birth rates, more people living to old age, and the graying of the seventy-six million boomer generation (people born in 1946–1964).

Trend 2—Changing Markers of Old Age. Age sixty-five is no longer the benchmark signaling the onset of late life. A person's chronological age no longer necessarily determines behavior and lifestyle. Images of the later years we remember from the past are no longer so clear. All across adulthood, chronological age has become a poor predictor of the timing of life events. Young people are waiting until much later to marry, have babies, and "settle down." Many boomers and older adults will continue to work well past "normal" retirement age. With longer life stages, there may be a stretching in years of childhood, adolescence, young adulthood, midlife, and old age. Do these "extra" years of life all have to come at the end, or could they help expand and stretch each stage throughout the life span?

Trend 3—Pandemic of Chronic Health Conditions. As more people live into the later years, society may be heading toward a future in which chronic health conditions become pervasive. Medical procedures and technology, scientific discoveries, lifestyles, drugs and medications are all helping people live longer, but will society experience increasing numbers of frail elderly? While there have been improved treatments for heart disease and cancer, which have significantly added disability-free life expectancy, dementia and neuro-degenerative disorders like Parkinson's disease and chronic disabling conditions like diabetes are a growing concern.

Trend 4—Increasingly Costly Health Care. Healthcare costs remain a significant drain on the budgets of older adults, and today, millions of people are without health insurance. Even with some form of health-care legislation by Congress, the United States will be one of the very few developed nations without universal health care. There is a growing divide in our society between the *well-derly* (wealthy) and *ill-derly* (poor) among older adults. With medical technology radically altering disease and health conditions related to aging and the increasing cost of health care, will battles erupt over who will decide how these technologies will be used and who will have access to them?

Trend 5—An Era of New Responsibility. The societal safety net for older adults is shrinking. Federal and state government support for older adults is strong, but it is under attack by the strain of expenses on all levels. This results in austerity measures that cut public spending on social services, causing cutbacks for all ages, including programs for older adults. Aging services will be most affected by the growing numbers of seniors. The focus will shift to mass prevention and diagnosis and to wellness aspects of the mind, body, and soul. In addition, perhaps as a result of the anti-aging industry, many people in our society are under the illusion that the limitations and suffering of older adults are not a natural part of life but a consequence of bad life management. Older adults are expected to take on more responsibility for the lifestyle choices they make. Their failure to age "successfully" may push them to the margins of society.

Trend 6—Family Caregiving Concerns. The role of the family in caregiving is important. However, there are some significant changes occurring in the traditional patterns of family life that affect the important role of caregiving. These include: fewer family members available to share in caregiving as a result of declines in birthrate and family size; divorce, remarriage, and blended families are changing family networks; lifestyle mobility is causing children to live at a great distance from their aging parents, bringing about a need for long-distance caregiving. In addition, there are competing responsibilities of caregiving. Grandparents are raising grandchildren at the same time one grandparent is caring for a frail spouse. Who will provide care for the large numbers of older adults?

Trend 7—Increase in Numbers of Older Adults with Dementia. Today, there are approximately five million people who have Alzheimer's Disease. By 2030, more than eight million Americans will be living with some form of dementia. The Alzheimer's Association projects that if there is no cure or medical advancement in delaying or eradicating the onset of Alzheimer's Disease by 2050, as many as fifteen million people could have the disease.[1] Rural America is being hit particularly hard. The migration of young people leaving farming communities coupled with the movement of retirees away from cities to pastoral settings is tipping rural demographics toward people age sixty-five and older. Rural communities will face the challenge of an aging population with increasing numbers of people living with dementia. What effect will this increase have on families, churches, and communities? It would be of great benefit to everyone if the church, particularly in rural settings, would take the lead in creating dementia-friendly communities where every part of the community plays a role and works together to create a dementia-friendly culture. For more information about dementia-friendly communities, see www.dfamerica.org/toolkit.

Trend 8—Financial Insecurity. The gift of long life also presents a financial challenge. How do people finance living into their eighties and nineties? Prior to Social Security (in 1935) and Medicare (in 1965), more than a third of older adults lived in poverty. With the advent of social insurance programs, the poverty rate for older adults in recent years dropped significantly. However, both federal and state budgets are changing, and resources for older adults are declining. What will the future hold? With challenges to Social Security and Medicare, changes in pension programs, and the bursting of the housing bubble, we could face a future with a growing increase in elder poverty. Some seniors will have more than enough resources to have a comfortable retirement, while others will barely be able to make it from day to day, let alone from month to month.

Trend 9—Changes in Retirement. Many people will continue to work long after the "normal" age of retirement. Often, older adults keep working because of continuing career interests, the desire to stay productive, fear of unstable Social Security coverage, loss of pensions or benefits, dwindling retirement investments; some simply can't afford to retire. But, whatever the reason, the trend seems to be shifting from early retirement to later retirement for many older adults.

Trend 10—Elder Abuse. As a result of increasing numbers of older adults, one can reasonably surmise that elder abuse will also increase. Exploitation of the elderly is presently an underreported problem. As the population ages, more older adults could become victims. Elder abuse may be in the form of neglect/self-neglect, psychological/emotional, financial, physical/sexual, and spiritual. The typical victim of elder abuse is a woman between the ages of seventy and eighty-nine who is frail and cognitively impaired. She may be lonely, isolated, and trusting of those who take an interest in her. Should more congregations spearhead "safe sanctuaries for elderly" and provide training for caregivers and volunteers who work with older adults?

Trend 11—Aging in Place. There are changes in how and where older adults live. The image of older adults living the end of their lives in nursing homes is a thing of the past. Use of nursing homes is declining, while there is an increase in home- and community-based services. In-home products and technology are making it easier for people with disabilities to live independently. Many public- and private-sector programs provide incentives for older adults to stay in their own homes for as long as possible, including reverse mortgages, businesses catering to homebound older adults, adult day programs, alternative planned housing developments where neighbors help neighbors, and multigenerational homes where adult children can live with their aging parents.

Trend 12—Technology and Aging. Technology is an aging game changer by improving older adults' independence, engagement, and health, and reducing their social isolation. Whether already in use or still being tested, aging-in-place technology is improving the aging experience for seniors and family caregivers. One of the exciting new technologies is the development of artificial intelligence, or AI, and "big data." With AI, devices can react like humans after assessing a situation and learning someone's habits. Wearable gadgets—think Fitbit on steroids—can collect and analyze health data, while medical mini-machines monitor chronic conditions and customize treatment. There may be "self-driving" (or driverless) cars where older adults will no longer have to give up their car keys, "humanized big data" that will help plan individualized medical treatments, and "second skin" that will restore natural elasticity and a youthful appearance. Transportation, medical, and health-care needs, housing and livable communities and family caregiving are just some of the many ways life will be affected by advances in technology and AI as we age.

Trend 13—Declining Church Participation. Previous generations of older adults had a relatively high percentage of their numbers participating in the life of the church. While it may be true that older adults become more "spiritual" as they age, it may not be true that older adults in the near future will become more "religious" as they age. With previous generations, older adults went to church as result of a faith commitment, and sometimes out of a sense of "obligation" or a belief that it was "good for business" to be seen in church. As we read in Chapter 5, baby boomers do not necessarily have the same inclination about church membership and attendance as did previous generations of older adults. The church will need to reach boomers in new ways to have their commitment and participation in the life of the church. In some cases, older adults are feeling disenfranchised by the church due to changes in worship styles and music or from a sense that the church does not care about their needs or spiritual well-being. And boomers are not "brand loyal" to the denomination in which they were raised. Growing numbers of older adults may already be leaving the church altogether or simply not attending worship services. According to recent reports, there are increasing numbers of young people who indicate that they have no affiliation with a particular church denomination or with religion. They are sometimes identified as the "nones." If this trend continues, churches will likely see an increase in the percentage of midlife and older adults who do not participate in the life of the church.

Conclusion

The chance to live longer has increased enormously over the years. More people are living into old age than ever before. Our society has never had so many older adults who are healthy, active, and gifted. We are engaged in an age of opportunity as older adults begin to imagine the possibilities for living a long life. And it is my hope that churches will experience this age of opportunity as a time to reimagine what church vitality can be with a graying congregation.

Because of these newly emerging trends, there is a great need for bold vision by faith leaders. The question for our time is not, "How can the church serve older adults?" but instead "How can the church embrace the gifts of aging people and create intentional ministry by, with, and for older adults?" A congregation with many older members will be offered more opportunities and unexpected challenges than ever imagined. It is important for congregations to neither devalue the exciting possibilities of an aging congregation nor hide the vulnerabilities of aging.

Since many of us will live longer and healthier lives than previous generations of older adults, we have the opportunity to create a second half of life that is fundamentally different from what our parents and grandparents experienced. However, we will also face new challenges and struggles as these trends suggest.

We need not deny our aging, but rather gain a new perspective of what it means to be people of great worth as older children of God. In reality, we are pioneers, forging new paths and definitions about what it means to be older adults. Let's not get bogged down by the trends but learn from them and fashion a faithful future. We've earned our wrinkles and our wisdom, and we possess the wonderful opportunity to grow closer to God through Jesus Christ and to our true selves. As the writer of Psalms suggests: "The righteous flourish like the palm tree, and grow like a cedar in Lebanon . . . In old age they still produce fruit; they are always green and full of sap" (Psalm 92:12, 14).

Facts about Aging Quiz— True or False

_____ 1. In general, most old people are pretty much alike.

_____ 2. Different parts of the body age at different rates.

_____ 3. The poverty rate level for older adults in 2015 was below fifteen percent.

_____ 4. Most older adults are set in their ways and unable to change.

_____ 5. Childlessness is a risk factor for social isolation among older adults.

_____ 6. In 2015, about one in every four, or 25 percent, of the population was an older adult, age sixty-five and older.

_____ 7. People reaching age sixty-five have an average life expectancy of approximately an additional twenty years.

_____ 8. Older men are much more likely to be married than older women.

_____ 9. The majority of older adults in the United States consider their health to be good, very good, or excellent.

_____ 10. The majority of older adults worry about death.

_____ 11. Almost half of all older women age seventy-five years and older live alone.

_____ 12. Racial and ethnic minority populations among older adults will increase in the United States to fifty percent of the older-adult population by 2030.

_____ 13. Less than four percent of older adults in the United States are living in nursing homes.

_____ 14. As a result of our aging population and graying congregations, United Methodist-related seminaries and divinity schools started requiring course work in gerontology for all students in 2017 as a result of action by General Conference in 2016.

_____ 15. As people grow older, their ability to learn decreases.

_____ 16. The major source of income for older adults is from Social Security.

_____ 17. The majority of old people (past 65 years) have Alzheimer's Disease.

_____ 18. Depression is a common emotional problem of older adults.

Facts about Aging Quiz— Answers

1. **False**—Older adults are perhaps the least homogeneous group of all age cohorts. On many levels, they are more diverse due to their varied health, social roles, economic opportunities, and coping experiences throughout their lives. As the older population becomes more and more ethnically diverse, differences could be even greater.

2. **True**—Age does not have a uniform effect on different organs of the body, even in the same individual. For example, the heart may show signs of aging faster than the lungs.

3. **True**—Over 4.2 million older adults (8.8 percent) were below the poverty level in 2015. In 2011, the U.S. Census Bureau released a new Supplemental Poverty Measure (SPM) that takes into account regional variations in living costs and medical out-of-pocket expenses. As a result, in 2015, the SPM shows a poverty level for older

adults of 13.7 percent (almost five percentage points higher than the official rate of 8.8 percent), but still below fifteen percent.

4. **False**—The majority of older adults are not "set in their ways and unable to change." There is some evidence that older people need continuity in their lives and tend to become more stable in their attitudes, but it is clear that older people do change. To survive, they must adapt to the many changes and transitions in later life, including such events as retirement, children leaving home, widowhood, moving to new homes, and serious illness.

5. **True**—Childlessness is an important risk factor for social isolation among older adults. While childless adults often do have support networks, usually consisting of relatives, friends, and neighbors, these systems are less likely to provide the long-term commitment and comparable high level of support that children give to parents.

6. **False**—In 2015, about one in every seven, or 14.9 percent of the population was sixty-five years of age and older.

7. **True**—Persons reaching age sixty-five have an average life expectancy of an additional 19.4 years (20.6 years for females and 18 years for males).

8. **True**—Older men are much more likely to be married than older women (70 percent of men; 45 percent of women).

9. **True**—More than seventy percent of older adults said their health was "good, very good, or excellent," while

less than thirty percent indicated that their health was "fair or poor."

10. **False**—Although death in our society has come to be associated primarily with old age, studies generally indicate that death anxiety in adults decreases as age increases. Some studies do indicate that there is a greater fear about dying than death itself.

11. **True**—Almost half of older women (46 percent) age seventy-five and older do live alone.

12. **False**—Racial and ethnic minority populations have increased from eighteen percent of the older adult population in 2005 to twenty-two percent in 2015. The projected increase in 2030 is twenty-eight percent of the older-adult population.

13. **True**—In 2015, 3.1 percent of the older-adult population lived in nursing homes or other institutional settings. However, the percentage increases dramatically with age, ranging (in 2015) from one percent for people sixty-five to seventy-four-years to three percent for people seventy-five to eighty-four years and nine percent for people who are eighty-five years and older.

14. **False**—Although there is steady growth in our aging population and among the membership in our churches, United Methodist-related seminaries and divinity schools do not require course work in gerontology, nor did General Conference in 2016 make any such proposal.

15. **False**—Although learning performance tends on average to decline with age, older adults can learn anything

if given adequate time, understanding, and circumstances. Research studies have shown that learning performances can be improved with instructions and practice, extra time to learn information or skills, and relevance of the learning task to interests and expertise.

16. **True**—The major sources of income as reported by older adults in 2014 were Social Security (reported by 84 percent of older adults), income from assets (62 percent), private pensions (37 percent), earnings (29 percent), and government employee pensions (16 percent).

17. **False**—According to the 2014 Alzheimer's Disease "Facts and Figures Report" published by the Alzheimer's Association, one in nine people sixty-five and older (11 percent) have Alzheimer's Disease. About one-third of people age eighty-five and older (32 percent) have Alzheimer's Disease.

18. **True**—Deaths of loved ones, decreased income, and failing health often lead to depression among older adults.

Creating a Survey Instrument

Two Types of Surveys: Questionnaire and Interview

1. Questionnaire—usually "paper and pencil" instruments or online that the respondent completes
2. Interview—usually completed by the interviewer based on the what the respondent says

Who

Whom do you want to survey? List everyone or every group or age cohort you want to include in your survey.

What

What do you want to know? Determine the content of the questions and the wording of each question, as well as your scope and purpose.

When

When do you want to do the survey? Indicate the time of year and the number of days, weeks, or months when you plan to gather the survey information.

How

How will you conduct the survey? Consider the response format you will use for collecting the information from the respondents. Indicate whether you will use Survey Monkey or another online tool. Indicate whether you will use the survey in person at church during church school or at other times or during direct visitation.

Where

Where will survey information be gathered? Indicate who is to receive the completed surveys and who will process the information.

Sample—Older-Adult Survey 1

1. Contact the person to be interviewed and establish a mutually agreed upon day and time for the interview. Visit in pairs (two people per team for each visit)
2. Upon arriving for the interview, identify yourself and briefly state the nature of your visit.
3. Give the person being interviewed a copy of this survey form, read each question aloud, and record the information on your form.

Name: _____

Address: _____

_____ **Telephone:** _____

Email: _____ **Date of Interview:** _____

1. Marital Status: ____ Single,   ____ Married,

____ Widowed,   ____ Divorced

2. Gender: ___ Female ___ Male **3. Birth date:** _____

4. Do you live alone? ___ Yes ___ No

    If No, with whom do you live: _____

    _____

5. In an emergency, is there someone to whom you could turn for assistance? ___ No ___ Yes: To whom: _____

6. During this past week, how many times did you:

    Have someone come to visit with you? _____

    Talk with a friend or relative on the phone? _____

    Go visit someone else? _____

7. How do you rate your overall health?

    ___ Excellent ___ Very Good ___ Good

    ___ Fair ___ Poor

8. What problems do you experience with where you live?

    _____

    (Check all that apply)

9. Transportation: I need transportation for:

    ___ Church Activities ___ Groceries

    ___ Drug Store ___ Doctor's Office

    ___ Others: _____

    I could help transport others to: _____

10. Minor Home Repair and Maintenance: I need help with:

_____ Plumbing _____ Painting _____ Carpentry

_____ Lawn Care _____ Moving items

_____ Other: _____

I could help others with home repairs: _____

11. Home Chore Service: I need help with:

_____ Laundry _____ Cooking _____ Cleaning

_____ Shopping _____ Other: _____

I could help others with home chores: _____

12. Health Care: I need help with:

_____ Medical care _____ Dental care

_____ Vision/Hearing

_____ Other: _____

I could help others with health care: _____

13. Legal and Financial Counsel: I need help with:

_____ Will Planning _____ Medicare/Medicaid

_____ Power of Attorney _____ Advance Directives

_____ Others: _____

I could help others with legal/financial advice: _____

14. Congregational Care: I need:

_____ Pastoral Visitation _____ Holy Communion

_____ Prayer _____ Lay Visitation

_____ Devotional Materials _____ Other: _____

I could help others with congregation care needs: _____

_____

To be completed by Interviewer:

Interviewer's Name: _____

Interviewer's Contact Information: _____

Telephone: _____ Email: _____

Sample—Older Adult Survey 2

Name: _____

Address: _____

_____

Phone #: _____ Email Address: _____

Gender: ❏ Female ❏ Male Date of Birth: _____

Marital Status: ❏ Married ❏ Single, Never Married

❏ Divorced ❏ Widowed

Do you live alone? ❏ Yes ❏ No

If no, with whom do you live? _____

In the event of an emergency, if you need help or became ill or disabled, is there someone to whom you could turn for assistance? ❏ Yes ❏ No

If yes, who? _____ Relationship: _____

Address: _____ Telephone # _____

During the past week, how many times did you:

Have someone visit you? ____ Visit someone else? ____

Go shopping? ____ Talk with a friend or relative on the telephone? ____

Do you experience any problems with where you live?

❑ Yes ❑ No

If yes, what are the problems? _____

Please rate your health: ❑ Excellent ❑ Very Good ❑ Good

❑ Fair ❑ Poor

Approximately how often do you attend religious services?

❑ Weekly ❑ Twice a month ❑ Monthly ❑ Quarterly

❑ Yearly ❑ Never

Would you like to receive any of the following religious services in your home?

❑ Pastoral Visitation ❑ Lay Visitation ❑ Devotional materials

❑ Bible study materials ❑ Holy Communion,

❑ Other: _____

Do You Need?			Can You Provide?	
❏ Yes	❏ No	Transportation	❏ Yes	❏ No
❏ Yes	❏ No	Home Repairs	❏ Yes	❏ No
❏ Yes	❏ No	Housekeeping Chores	❏ Yes	❏ No
❏ Yes	❏ No	Minor Plumbing Repairs	❏ Yes	❏ No
❏ Yes	❏ No	Minor Carpentry Repairs	❏ Yes	❏ No
❏ Yes	❏ No	Legal Counsel	❏ Yes	❏ No
❏ Yes	❏ No	Income Tax Preparation	❏ Yes	❏ No
❏ Yes	❏ No	Financial Counsel	❏ Yes	❏ No
❏ Yes	❏ No	Medical Assistance	❏ Yes	❏ No
❏ Yes	❏ No	Meal Preparation	❏ Yes	❏ No
❏ Yes	❏ No	Reading Materials	❏ Yes	❏ No
❏ Yes	❏ No	Support Group	❏ Yes	❏ No
❏ Yes	❏ No	Fellowship Group	❏ Yes	❏ No
❏ Yes	❏ No	Bible Study Group	❏ Yes	❏ No
❏ Yes	❏ No	Prayer Group	❏ Yes	❏ No
❏ Yes	❏ No	Caregivers Support Group	❏ Yes	❏ No
❏ Yes	❏ No	Respite Support	❏ Yes	❏ No
❏ Yes	❏ No	Travel Opportunities	❏ Yes	❏ No

Other Need(s) You Have: _____

_____

_____

Other Ministry You Can Provide: _____

_____

_____

Please identify or list any programs the church (or seniors' group) should provide for older adults: _____

Name of Interviewer: _____ Date: _____

Sample—Older-Adult Survey 3

1. Contact the older person to be interviewed and establish a mutually agreed upon day and time for the interview. Visit in pairs (two people per team for each visit).
2. Upon arriving for the interview, identify yourself and briefly state the nature of your visit.
3. Give the person being interviewed a copy of this survey form, read each question aloud, and record the information on your form.

Section I: Contact Information

Name of older member being interviewed: _____

Address of older member: _____

_____

Phone # of Member: _____

Email Address: _____

1. Age: _____ 2. Birth date: _____

3. Gender: Female _____ Male _____

4. Race/Ethnicity (optional): _____

Did other(s) participate in interview or speak for member?

Yes _____ No _____

(If Yes) Name: _____ Relationship: _____

(If Yes) Name: _____ Relationship: _____

Section II: Life Story

5. Invite member to share aspects of his/her life: _____

_____

_____

_____

_____

_____

_____

Section III: Current Demographics

6. Living Arrangement:

_____ Independent w/spouse or partner in own home

_____ Independent alone in own home

_____ Living with another person in the home

_____ Living in co-housing setting

_____ Living in an assisted-living facility

_____ Living in a nursing home or continuing care retirement center

_____ Other: _____

7. Mobility Status: _____ Go-Go (Active); _____ Slow-Go (Passive); _____ No-Go (Final)

Explain: _____

_____

Section IV: Attitudes, Interests, & Opinions

8. What could your church offer to make your life better?

A. _____

B. _____

C. _____

D. _____

9. What things do you like most to do that bring joy to your life?

A. _____

B. _____

C. _____

D. _____

10. Is the church doing enough of the right things to serve the needs of older members?

A. _____

B. _____

C. _____

D. _____

Name of Interviewer: _____ Date: _____

Interviewer post-interview comments and observations: ____

_____

_____

Conducting an Older-Adult Survey Interview

1. Design a survey form to gather the information you want concerning the needs and talents of older adults in your community.
2. Determine the people you want to survey. Who are your older adults? 65 years of age and older? Where do they reside?
3. Announce plans for conducting the survey from the pulpit and through the weekly worship bulletin and church newsletter.
4. Select as many teams of two as possible. Invite mature youth and young adults, as well as other adults, to participate in conducting the survey.
5. Select a time to meet together with your visiting teams at the church.

- Provide each team with a clipboard, pencil, and survey forms.
- Review the survey together.
- Provide instructions for conducting the interview.
- Agree on people to be visited.
- Provide names, addresses, and phone numbers of survey participants.
- Encourage each team to contact survey participants prior to conducting the survey and to set up a day and time to conduct the survey interview.
- If necessary, provide name tags for teams to wear that clearly identify the interviewers and the name of your church.

6. When conducting the survey interview,
   - Be prompt in visiting the survey participant at the agreed-on day and time.
   - Introduce yourself, show identification, and state why you are there.
   - Give the older adult being interviewed a copy of the survey form.
   - Ask each question on the form and write or print each answer clearly.
   - Do not overextend your stay.
   - Thank the survey participant for taking the time to complete the survey form.

7. Each team should return the survey forms to the church.

8. Arrange for a small group to collate the material.

9. Enter the information received into a database and begin a file on each person
10. Send a thank-you note to all older adults who participated in the survey. Give the general results of the survey, such as number of homes contacted, the three most mentioned needs, and so on.

SUGGESTED RESOURCES FOR FURTHER READING AND STUDY

Ageing and Spirituality across Faiths and Cultures edited by Elizabeth MacKinlay. Jessica Kingsley Publishers, London, UK (2010). This collection of essays examines aging in the context of the many faiths and cultures that make up Western society.

Agewise: Fighting the New Ageism in America by Margaret Morganroth Gullette. University of Chicago Press, Chicago, IL (2011). By examining the ageism in our society, the author provides a clear and convincing call for a movement of resistance.

Aging and Ministry in the 21st Century by Richard H. Gentzler, Jr. Discipleship Resources, Nashville, TN (2008). This book provides an inquiry approach to individual or small-group study concerning aging issues and their impact on ministry.

Aging and the Art of Living by Jan Baars. The Johns Hopkins University Press, Baltimore, MD (2012). The author compares and contrasts ancient and modern societal views of aging.

Aging as a Spiritual Practice by Lewis Richmond. Gotham Books, New York, NY (2012). A user's guide to aging well and making every year fulfilling and transformative.

Aging Matters: Finding Your Calling for the Rest of Your Life by R. Paul Stevens. William B. Eerdmans Publishing Company, Grand Rapids, MI (2016). The author proposes that our calling does not end with formal retirement but that we must continue to discern our vocation as we grow older.

Aging Nation: The Economics and Politics of Growing Older in America by James H. Schulz and Robert H. Binstock. Praeger Publishers, Westport, CT (2006). A solid corrective look at the conventional (and often false) wisdom, propagated by the doomsters, about the perils of a nation living longer.

Basic Ministry for the Second Half of Life by Robert W. Chism. Inspiring Voices, Bloomington, IN (2012). The author serves as a guide and provides resources and spiritual insight into the second half of life.

Baby Boomers and Beyond by Amy Hanson. Jossey-Bass, San Francisco, CA (2010). The author explores the opportunities and challenges that the older adult population presents to the Christian community.

Being Mortal: Medicine and What Matters in the End by Atul Gawande. Metropolitan Books, New York (2014).

The author, a practicing surgeon, shows how the ultimate goal is not a good death but a good life—all the way to the very end.

The Big Shift: Navigating the New Stage Beyond Midlife by Marc Freedman. Public Affairs, New York, NY (2011). The author provides guidelines for living into a new stage of life between the middle years and the beginning of old age.

Boomer Spirituality: Seven Values for the Second Half of Life by Craig Kennet Miller. Discipleship Resources, Nashville, TN (2017). The author provides a valuable resource for clearly understanding the unique spirituality of the boomer generation.

Caresharing by Marty Richards. Skylight Paths Publishing, Woodstock, VT (2009). The author provides a clear understanding of a reciprocal approach to caregiving and care receiving as people face the complexities of aging, illness, and disability.

Celebrating the Rest of Your Life: A Baby Boomer's Guide to Spirituality by David Yount. Augsburg Books, Minneapolis, MN (2005). A valuable resource to help boomers find meaning and satisfaction in the retirement years.

The Church Responds to Abuse, Neglect, and Exploitation of Older Adults by Joy Thornburg Melton. Discipleship Resources, Nashville, TN (2012). The author provides a clear understanding of elder abuse and a helpful guide for church ministry.

Creative Aging: Rethinking Retirement and Non-Retirement in a Changing World by Marjory Zoet Bankson. Skylight Paths Publishing, Woodstock, VT (2010). The author provides practical and useful ways for exploring the spiritual dimensions of retirement and aging.

Designing an Older Adult Ministry by Richard H. Gentzler, Jr. Discipleship Resources, Nashville, TN (2006). A "how-to" and informative resource for organizing and sustaining an intentional ministry by, with, and for older adults in local church settings.

Dimensions of Older Adult Ministry: A Handbook edited by Richard L. Morgan. Witherspoon Press, Presbyterian Church (USA), Louisville, KY (2006). This resource provides basic information about the aging process and older adult ministries.

Don't Write My Obituary Just Yet by Missy Buchanan. Upper Room Books, Nashville, TN (2011). Using inspiring faith stories by older adults, the author invites the reader to learn and grow in faith.

Ending Ageism or How Not to Shoot Old People by Margaret Morganroth Gullette. Rutgers University Press, New Brunswick, NJ (2017). This book effectively addresses ageism and powerfully argues that overcoming ageism is the next imperative social movement of our time.

Falling Upward: A Spirituality for the Two Halves of Life by Richard Rohr. Jossey-Bass, San Francisco, CA (2011). The author contemplates how our failings can be the foundation for our ongoing spiritual growth.

The Gift of Years by Joan D. Chittister. BlueBridge, New York, NY (2008). The author invites the reader to examine the purpose of our later years and to experience the gift of these years as not merely being alive, but as the gift of becoming more fully alive.

Golden Cross Foundation Grant Application and Guidelines, https://www.goldencrossfoundation.org/application-guidelines/

The grant guidelines and application are only for local United Methodist churches in the Tennessee Conference. The purpose of sharing this information is to provide an example for other religious entities and judicatory bodies that might want to create grant funding opportunities for older-adult ministries within their jurisdictions.

Healthy Aging: A Lifelong Guide to Your Physical and Spiritual Well-Being by Andrew Weil, M.D. Alfred A. Knopf, New York (2005). This book suggests that although aging is an irreversible process, there are myriad things we can do to keep our minds and bodies in good working order through all phases of life.

How to Minister Among Older Adults by Charles T. Knippel. Concordia Publishing House, St. Louis, MO (2005). This manual explores the many options for ministry with and to the older-adult age group. Also included are planning forms to start or expand an older-adult ministry program.

Jewish Visions for Aging: A Professional Guide for Fostering Wholeness by Rabbi Dayle A. Friedman. Jewish Lights Publishing, Woodstock, VT (2008). This rich resource uses Jewish texts to offer solutions and suggestions for finding meaning, purpose, and community in aging.

A Journey Called Aging: Challenges and Opportunities in Older Adulthood by James C. Fisher and Henry C. Simmons. Haworth Press, Binghamton, NY (2007). A useful resource in helping older adults plan their own journey through the later years.

Joyfully Aging: A Christian's Guide by Richard Bimler. Concordia Publishing House, St. Louis, MO (2012). The author, through brief stories and meditations, provides ways to celebrate God's gift of aging.

Living Fully, Dying Well by Bishop Rueben P. Job. Abingdon Press, Nashville, TN (2006). This study, which contains a workbook, leader's guide, and video, is designed to assist people in making careful, wise, and prayerful preparation for meeting life's most important moments.

A Long Bright Future: Happiness, Health, and Financial Security in an Age of Increased Longevity by Laura L. Carstenses. Public Affairs, New York, NY (2011). The author provides a vision for new possibilities offered by a longer life by focusing on finances, health, and social relationships.

The Longevity Economy by Joseph Coughlin. Public Affairs, New York, NY (2017). Although the author addresses issues concerning the growing aging population and what actions businesses should take, church leaders can gain valuable insight into planning congregational ministry with the graying of our churches.

Marketing to Leading-Edge Baby Boomers by Brent Green. Paramount Market Publishing, Ithaca, NY (2005). This resource provides valuable information and insight for congregational leaders who are seeking to reach baby boomers.

Ministry to and with the Elderly by Timothy M. Farabaugh. Authorhouse, Bloomington, IN (2005). A resource that not only provides information about the unique needs of older adults but provides examples and ways both clergy and elderly may be involved in ministry with older adults.

Ministering to Older Adults: The Building Blocks, edited by Donald R. Koepke. Haworth Press, Binghamton, NY (2005). This resource provides a step-by-step approach for designing a congregational-based ministry with older adults.

Never Say Die: The Myth and Marketing of the New Old Age by Susan Jacoby. Pantheon Books, New York, NY (2011). The author takes an honest and realistic look at aging and contends that our society is engaged in willful denial about old age.

No Act of Love Is Ever Wasted by Jane Marie Thibault and Richard L. Morgan. Upper Room Books, Nashville, TN (2009). The authors provide a thoughtful and compassionate look at issues of relevance to people concerned about and struggling with dementia.

Older Americans, Vital Communities: A Bold Vision for Societal Aging by W. Andrew Achenbaum. The Johns Hopkins University Press, Baltimore, MD (2005). A valuable resource that addresses various societal issues of aging.

Our Help in Ages Past: The Black Church's Ministry Among the Elderly by Bobby Joe Saucer with Jean Alicia Elster. Judson Press, Valley Forge, PA (2005). This resource challenges and engages black churches (Baptist) in developing intentional ministry among older adults.

Pilgrimage into the Last Third of Life by Jane Marie Thibault and Richard L. Morgan. Upper Room Books, Nashville, TN (2012). The authors provide Scripture-based meditations and reflections on how people can spend the God-gift of a longer life.

Retire to a Better You by Ed Zinkiewicz. Retirement-U, Inc. (2013). The author, through a series of helpful "retire to" books, this being one of them, provides encouragement, hope, and meaning for people in the retirement years.

Seasons of Caring: Meditations for Alzheimer's and Dementia Caregivers edited by Dr. Daniel C. Potts, Lynda Everman, Rabbi Steven M. Glazer, Dr. Richard L. Morgan, and Max Wallack. ClergyAgainstAlzheimer's Network, 2014. A wonderful resource for spiritual support that is filled with stories, reflections, and meditations for caregivers from various faith traditions.

Second Wind: Navigating the Passage to a Slower, Deeper, and More Connected Life by Dr. Bill Thomas. Simon & Schuster, New York, NY (2014). The author provides an in-depth understanding in how to recognize the challenges and to navigate the second half of life.

Settling In: My First Year in a Retirement Community by Richard H. Morgan. Upper Room Books, Nashville, TN (2006). Through Scripture, prayers, and brief meditations, Morgan addresses the fears of the retirement years, including loss of health, loss of cognitive ability, and loss of social status.

Shaping a Life of Significance for Retirement by R. Jack Hansen and Jerry P. Haas. Upper Room Books, Nashville, TN (2010). The authors provide helpful suggestions for retirees to reflect on their living in an effort to make the later years very fulfilling years.

Soul Unfinished: Finding Happiness, Taking Risks, and Trusting God as We Grow Older by Robert Atwell. Paraclete Press, Brewster, MA (2012). The author provides insight and guidance to the reader in living life to the fullest potential in old age.

Spirituality and Aging by Robert C. Atchley. The Johns Hopkins University Press, Baltimore, MD (2009). The author, separating spirituality from religion, provides a nuanced view of spirituality and the impact it has on the lives of older adults.

The Spirituality of Age: A Seeker's Guide to Growing Older by Robert L. Weber and Carol Orsborn. Park Street Press, Rochester, VT (2015). The authors guide the reader through a series of questions that provide understanding to the spiritual opportunities in aging and growing older.

Talking with God in Old Age by Missy Buchanan. Upper Room Books, Nashville, TN (2010). Through meditations and the use of Psalms, the author sensitively addresses the worries, fears, and frustrations of older adults.

Third Calling: What are you doing the rest of your life? by Richard and Leona Bergstrom. Church Health, Edmonds, Washington (2016). The authors provide readers with an excellent resource that can lead to a third calling in life filled with clarity, hope, faith, and meaning.

This Chair Rocks: A Manifesto Against Ageism by Ashton Applewhite. Networked Books (2016). The author provides a call to wake up to the ageism in society and within ourselves and to embrace a more nuanced and accurate view of growing older.

The Three Secrets of Aging: A Radical Guide by John C. Robinson. O-Books, Winchester, UK (2012). This helpful resource outlines the profound spiritual possibilities of aging and guides the reader in psychology, spirituality, and mysticism of life's final chapters.

Voices of Aging: Adult Children and Aging Parents Talk with God by Missy Buchanan. Upper Room Books, Nashville, TN (2015). The author offers a compassionate look at adult children and their aging parents as they face the fears and frustrations of aging.

With Purpose: Going from Success to Significance in Work and Life by Ken Dychtwald and Daniel J. Kadlec. HarperCollins Publishers, New York, NY (2009). The authors describe how the definition of success changes as you grow older and what you can do to make a difference in the world as you age.

ABOUT THE AUTHOR

The Rev. Dr. Richard H. Gentzler, Jr. (Rick) is the director of ENCORE Ministries, a ministry funded by the Golden Cross Foundation of the Tennessee Conference of The United Methodist Church. He is retired as a clergy member from the Susquehanna Annual Conference and is the former director of the Center on Aging and Older-Adult Ministries for the General Board of Discipleship (now called Discipleship Ministries) of The United Methodist Church.

Dr. Gentzler is an internationally recognized leader in the field of aging, midlife, and older-adult ministries. In 2013, he was selected by Governor Haslam to serve on the Governor's Task Force on Aging for the state of Tennessee. He was a keynote presenter for Conferences on Aging and Older Adult Ministries in Australia and New Zealand in 2013; a recipient of the *"Outstanding Leadership in Older Adult Ministries Award"* from the United Methodist Committee on Older Adult Ministries in 2012; a recipient of the *"Spirituality and Aging Award"* from the National Council on Aging (NCOA) and National Interfaith Coalition on Aging (NICA) in 2003; and in 2002 served as a presenter on spirituality and aging at the United Nations Second World Assembly on Ageing in

Madrid, Spain. In 2005 he produced the award-winning video on aging titled, *New Beginnings: The Gifts of Aging.*

Dr. Gentzler is a member of the board of directors for the Council on Aging of Middle Tennessee and serves as the board president. He is a resource consultant for both the Golden Cross Foundation of the Tennessee Conference and the Tennessee Conference Committee on Adult/Older-Adult Ministries.

Dr. Gentzler has been in ministry for more than forty-five years. He pastored churches in Pennsylvania and Maryland and taught classes at Lycoming College (Williamsport, PA), Wesley Theological Seminary (Washington, DC), Asbury Theological Seminary (Wilmore, KY), Union Presbyterian Seminary (Richmond, VA), and Lipscomb University (Nashville, TN).

Dr. Gentzler is author and co-author of numerous books on aging, midlife and older adults including:

- *Aging & Ministry in the 21st Century*
- *Aging: God's Challenge to Church and Synagogue*
- *The Graying of the Church*
- *Designing an Older Adult Ministry*
- *Gen2Gen: Sharing Jesus with All Generations*
- *Forty-Sixty: A Guide for Midlife Adults Who Want to Make a Difference*

Dr. Gentzler holds the following degrees: Bachelor of Science in Social Science/Secondary Education from Shippensburg University (Shippensburg, PA), Master of Divinity from Wesley Theological Seminary (Washington,

DC), Doctor of Ministry from Boston University School of Theology (Boston, MA), and a Certificate in Aging Studies from Boston University Institute for Geriatric Social Work. He is married to the former Marilyn Ann Hozyash. They have two married children, Dr. Richard Henry III (Emily) and Elizabeth, Esq. (Jennifer) and two grandchildren, Katherine and Richard Henry IV.

ENDNOTES

Introduction

1. *A Profile of Older Americans: 2016* by the Administration on Aging, Administration for Community Living, U.S. Department of Health and Human Services, pages 1-3, https://www.giaging .org/documents/A_Profile_of_Older_Americans__2016.pdf.
2. United States Census Bureau, "The Nation's Older Population Is Still Growing, Census Bureau Report," (News Release: CB17-100, June 22, 2017), https://www.census.gov/newsroom /press-releases/2017/cb17-100.html.

Chapter 1

1. *A Profile of Older Americans: 2016* by the Administration on Aging, Administration for Community Living, U.S. Department of Health and Human Services, page 2, https://www.giaging .org/documents/A_Profile_of_Older_Americans__2016.pdf.
2. *A Profile of Older Americans: 2016*, 1.
3. *A Profile of Older Americans: 2016*, 1.
4. United States Census Bureau, "The Changing Economics and Demographics of Young Adulthood From 1975-2016" (News Release CB17-TPS.36, April 1, 2017), https://www.census.gov /newsroom/press-releases/2017/cb17-tps36-young-adulthood .html.

5. New International Version (NIV) Holy Bible, New International Version®, NIV® Copyright ©1973, 1978, 1984, 2011 by Biblica, Inc.® Used by permission. All rights reserved worldwide.

Chapter 2

1. Mark Mather, Linda A. Jacobsen, and Kelvin M. Pollard, "Aging in the United States," Population Bulletin 70, no. 2 (2015), 13.
2. Mather, Jacobsen, and Pollard, *Population Bulletin.* Vol. 70, no. 2 (2015).
3. *A Profile of Older Americans: 2016* published by Administration on Aging, Administration for Community Living, U.S. Department of Health and Human Services, page 5.
4. *A Profile of Older Americans: 2016*, 5.

Chapter 4

1. CQ Researcher, A Division of Congressional Quarterly, Inc., Oct. 19, 2007, Volume 17, Number 37, pages 865-888, www.cq researcher.com.
2. *Marketing to Leading-Edge Baby Boomers* by Brent Green (Ithaca, NY: Paramount Market Publishing, Inc., 2005), 4.

Chapter 8

1. E. H. Erikson, *Childhood and Society* (New York: Norton, 1950). See also E. H. Erikson, *The Life Cycle Completed* (New York: Norton, 1985).

Chapter 10

1. 2017 Alzheimer's Disease Facts and Figures, https://www.alz .org.